Shruthi Harikrishna

The Store of Life

How to Fill Your Basket with Contentment

Om Books International

First published in 2025 by

Om Books International

Corporate & Editorial Office
A-12, Sector 64, Noida 201 301
Uttar Pradesh, India
Phone: +91 120 477 4100
Email: editorial@ombooks.com
Website: www.ombooksinternational.com

Sales Office
107, Ansari Road, Darya Ganj,
New Delhi 110 002, India
Phone: +91 11 4000 9000
Email: sales@ombooks.com
Website: www.ombooks.com

Text and artwork © Shruthi Harikrishna 2025

The views and opinions expressed in this book are those of the author, and have been verified to the extent possible, and the publishers are in no way liable for the same. No part of this book may be reproduced or transmitted in any form by any means, electronic or mechanical, including photocopying and recording, or by any information storage and retrieval system, except as may be expressly permitted in writing by the publisher.

Design and layout: Mohd Arif

ISBN: 978-93-6395-771-8

Printed in India

10 9 8 7 6 5 4 3 2 1

Shruthi Harikrishna is proof that spreadsheets and sketches can peacefully coexist. A state rank holder, a computer science engineer and an MBA from IIM Bangalore, she spends her days making sense of numbers and solving problems in her role handling analytics at a global software giant. But it is after-hours when she explores the lighter, more whimsical side of life through words, art and humour.

Her blog, TameShru@Wordpress, with over 20,000 views (a delightful surprise to her!), was where she first started sharing her quirky take on everyday life. She also dabbles in storytelling, with her short story winning the Deccan Herald Short Story competition in 2014. When she is not writing, you will find her creating intricate zentangles on Whorls_of_Maya or sharing quirky doodles on Doodle. Doodle. Do—both spaces that she considers her creative playgrounds.

Whether it is a blog, a doodle, or a story, Shruthi aims to make the heart smile, the brain tickle and life feel a little lighter—if only for a moment. This book is her way of blending her love for storytelling and problem-solving into a light-hearted guide to managing life's ups and downs.

Shruthi credits her daughter for being the embodiment of everything she preaches—living with unfiltered joy, curiosity and a knack for finding zen even in the most chaotic moments. Her ever-patient husband, who serves as her first reader and, often, the good-natured subject of her humour, continues to be her steadfast cheerleader. She is immensely grateful to her parents, who clap the loudest for her successes and show her every day what unconditional love truly means. For Shruthi, life is about finding joys in the small things and sharing a smile wherever she can.

You can take her out of a story, but you can't take the story out of her.

To

Puttani battani, Ro, Amma and Pappa—you fill my basket with boundless contentment

Contents

Foreword ix

Welcome to the Store of Life! xi

1.	How to Fill Your Basket of Life	1
2:	Think in esreveR	12
3.	Enjoy the Many Flavours of Saying NO	22
4.	Sow the Seeds of Learning	33
5.	The Compounding Effect of Habits	49
6.	Ask for Help	60
7.	Learn to Delegate	67
8.	Get Things Done	81
9.	Maintain a Balanced Diet for the Body, Mind and Soul	94

10.	Eat Mindfully	102
11.	Create Space	109
12.	Declutter Your Life	115
13.	Find What You Are Looking For	140
14.	Get Better with ~~Prastice Practise~~ Practice	145
15.	Disconnect to Stay Connected	154
16.	Stay in the Here and Now	162
17.	Find Joy in Everyday Happiness	172
18.	Realise Life Is Not a Zero-Sum Game	184
19.	Stay Contented	192

| Checking Out | 198 |
| *Acknowledgements* | 207 |

Foreword

When Shruthi asked me to write this foreword, I did what any self-respecting adult does when faced with a responsibility: I felt overwhelmed by it. Overwhelmed because I had never written a foreword to a book before. And writing one for such an unusually scripted book was particularly daunting. After procrastinating for as long as I could, and after having read the book end to end a couple of times, I finally felt armed with enough insights to introduce the book to its intended readers.

So, here's the thing—*The Store of Life* isn't your usual self-help book that preaches from a pedestal. It is more like a good friend who gently nudges you and says, "Hey, maybe you've been overthinking this life thing. Let's simplify." Shruthi weaves together wisdom, doodles and plenty of relatable moments to remind us that life is, at its core, a series of small, conscious choices. And if you have been lugging around more clutter (both physical and emotional) than you care to admit, this book might just be the wake-up call you didn't know you needed.

The beauty of this book is in its simplicity. It doesn't insist that you overhaul your life overnight. Instead, it asks you to peek into your basket of life, chuck out the expired envy, guilt and anger, and make space for what really matters—peace, purpose, joy and perhaps a little bit of chocolate (because balance matters, right?).

Many people tell you what should be done, but leave you bewildered as to how to do it. For example, many life coaches and gurus will tell you to "live in the moment". But no one tells you how! This is where the book surprises you with its freshness. Shruthi has a knack for breaking down big ideas into bite-sized nuggets that are easy to digest and, more importantly, to act on. Whether it is learning the art of saying "no" without feeling guilty or rediscovering the joy of being present at the moment, this book offers plenty of "aha" moments wrapped in humour, wit and wisdom. After all, the devil maybe in the detail, but simplicity is divine!

As you pick up this book, imagine yourself strolling through life's aisles with a basket that is lighter, more purposeful and full of fun. Because at the end of the day, isn't that what we're all striving for? So let Shruthi guide you with her delightful humour and no-nonsense wisdom. Just remember, the checkout line comes for us all, so pick wisely.

Here's to your journey—and may your basket always be filled with the good stuff.

Sandeep Dhar
Founder, Aidiator; Ex-CEO Tesco India; Ex-MD and India Consumer Banking Head, Goldman Sachs

Welcome to the Store of Life!

Welcome, my dear reader, to the beginning of your journey of discovering this book and thank you for choosing to read it. It is meant to be a potpourri of philosophy, spirituality and practical tips to managing your life better. I hope it tickles and stimulates your mind and makes your heart smile.

The Store of Life holds aisles that make you pause, reflect, and fill your basket with clarity and intent. Each lane nudges you to think, act, and evolve.

Thinking shapes your perspective, doing transforms intentions into action, and becoming is the quiet unfolding of who you truly are. Life is like a marketplace, filled with endless choices, each shaping the path ahead. The way you fill your basket—your thoughts, actions and habits—determines what you take home with you at the end of each day. This book invites you to browse through these aisles with curiosity, reflection and an openness to pick what nourishes your soul and leave behind what no longer serves you.

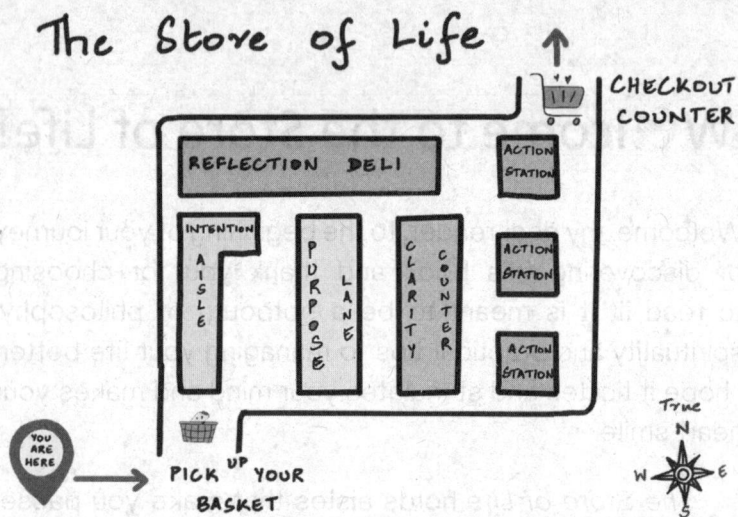

Every chapter is written with the aim of making you pause and reflect about the topic at hand, pushing you to make some commitments to yourself and inspiring you to become a better version of yourself.

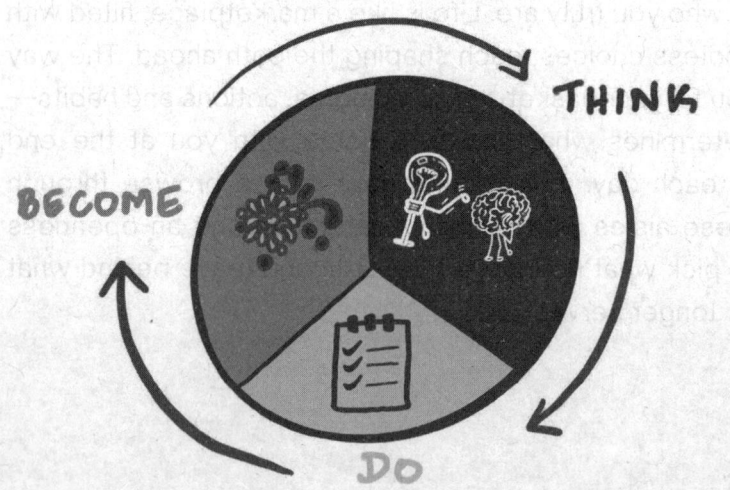

Pick up Your Basket

While reading this book, imagine stepping into the bustling store of life, where every chapter is a distinct aisle brimming with tools, ideas and inspiration to help you make the most out of your limited and precious time and energy. As you pick up your shopping basket, know that you can meander at your leisure, selecting what resonates with you and leaving the rest for another visit.

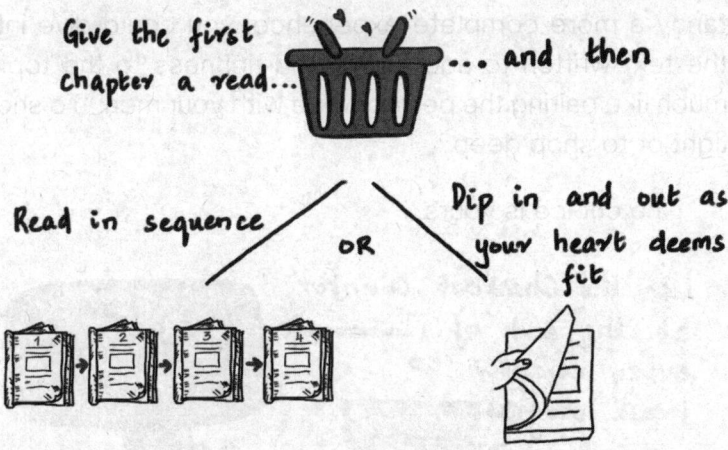

Just as in life, where your basket changes with circumstances, priorities and different stages, so too in this book, you will see many versions of the basket—each reflecting the evolving nature of what we carry. After all, change is the only constant in life. What fills your basket today may not serve you tomorrow, and that is perfectly okay. The beauty lies in embracing the ebb and flow, and curating your journey with intention and authenticity.

Whether you are here for a quick "life hack" snack or a full-on personal growth meal plan, every shelf is stocked with value.

Every chapter is like a well-stocked shelf, filled with doodles accompanied with text. You could simply browse through the pictures, like grabbing the essentials for a quick shop, and get the gist of the chapter. Or, if you fancy a more complete experience, you could dive into the text written to add depth and richness to the topic, much like pairing the perfect wine with your meal. To shop light or to shop deep?

The choice is yours.

Use the Checkout Counter at the end of every chapter to track progress made on your commitments

At the end of every chapter, you will find a checkout counter—your chance to bag up the key takeaways and take actionable steps to implement what you have learned. This section isn't just a formality; it is where you convert browsing into buying, *turning insights into real change*. Be sure to give it your attention and jot down your thoughts, just like keeping a receipt of your journey. These notes will serve as a record of your progress, letting you reflect on the past and gauge your progress.

It is time to grab your shopping basket and dive into the aisles of possibility.

To shop or not to shop?

That is not even up for debate! Happy shopping, and here's to filling your trolley with everything you need—and maybe a few delightful surprises along the way!

1
How to Fill Your  Of Life

Is shopping a joyous adventure, a treasure hunt filled with excitement and possibilities, or a necessary evil endured with grim determination and a mental stopwatch?

Whichever camp you belong to, one thing is certain. At some point in your life, you must have stepped into a

store, navigated its aisles and come out with exactly what you needed—or a trolley full of things you did not plan for but somehow could not resist buying.

In the traditional mode of shopping, the shopper has one finite resource: *money*. The shopper wants to maximise the number of items her money can buy her.

Now, what if life were a shopping experience too?

What if we were all given baskets the moment we were born, and the goal was to fill them up with items that we valued as we journeyed along the store of life? In this store too, we have one finite resource—time—and we aim to maximise our contentment, given the finite resource.

Every shopper is born with just one item in her basket—survival. The shopper pays dearly for this one item with screams, bawls, shrieks and howls.

As the shopper wanders down the aisle of adolescence, her eyes are drawn to an array of tempting items: learnings, hobbies, friendships and romance(s), each more alluring than the last. With limited time to spend, she knows she must choose wisely to maximise her contentment.

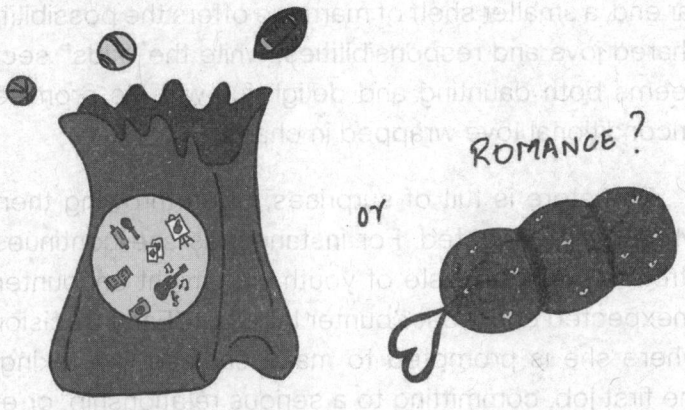

Do I really need such a large bag of hobbies when I could pick that soft, mushy red bag of romance instead? she muses. Every choice she makes shapes her basket, a reflection of what she values most in this fleeting stage of life.

Or perhaps she decides, "I want to fill my basket with every box of learning this store offers. There is always time to come back and pick up the other items later." With a determined stride, she begins stacking her basket with courses, degrees, books and skills—each one a new gateway to a better understanding of the self and the universe.

As she moves into the aisle of youth, the choices become even more enticing. She is met with counters brimming with love, marriage, passion, career, kids and money. A neatly packaged bundle of love promises companionship and adventures, while the career section boasts of exciting opportunities leading to success. At the far end, a smaller shelf of marriage offers the possibility of shared joys and responsibilities, while the "kids" section seems both daunting and delightful, with its promise of unconditional love wrapped in chaos.

The store is full of surprises, often throwing them in when least expected. For instance, as she continues to stroll through the aisle of youth, she might encounter an unexpected checkout counter labelled "Early Decisions", where she is prompted to make choices like taking up the first job, committing to a serious relationship, or even

moving abroad. Others may find this counter in middle age instead, with products bundled differently—perhaps a career change paired with parenting tips or a starter kit for reinvention.

And then there is the old-age section, often quieter but filled with its own charm. Here, the shelves display items like peace, reflection and wisdom, bundled neatly with time to enjoy the fruits of earlier purchases. She might discover discounted bundles labelled "Forgiveness" or "Legacy", reminding her to settle unfinished business or create a lasting impact.

Products often vary based on timing. The love and romance section in youth might feature whirlwind adventures and passionate sparks, while in middle age, the packaging shifts to long-term companionship and stability. Even hobbies look different depending on when she visits—the youthful shelves might offer adrenaline-pumping activities like skydiving or marathon running, while the later aisles highlight gardening or reading, This is not to generalise though, for how often have we seen senior citizens literally giving younger folks a "run" for their money?

And the time of the year matters too. Around New Year, the store prominently displays resolutions with bundles of health, fitness and goal-setting tools. During holidays, the counters overflow with family-time bundles, wrapped in love and togetherness. No two visits to the store are ever the same, and every choice adds its unique flavour to her journey.

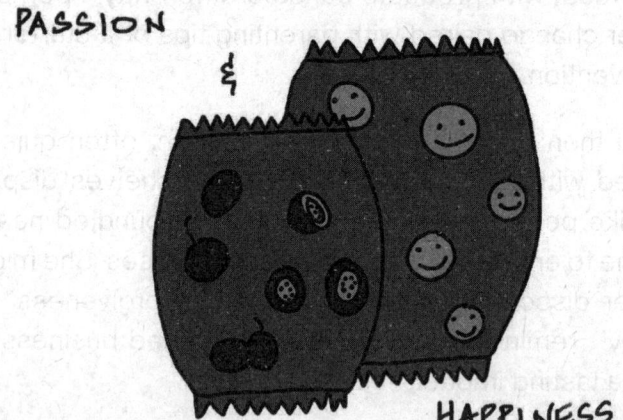

Similarly, in the store of life, many items often come bundled together, offering both opportunities and challenges. For instance, passion is frequently paired with happiness, creating a dynamic bundle that fuels both personal fulfilment and a sense of purpose. But alongside the joy of pursuing one's dreams, the package might also include long hours, uncertainty or sacrifices, making the choice even more significant.

Likewise, fame might be bundled with a mix of admiration and scrutiny. The shiny packaging promises recognition and influence yet hidden in the fine print are challenges like public expectations, loss of privacy and the pressure to maintain an image. It is a bundle many admire from afar but hesitate to add to their basket when they see the full picture.

On the other hand, spirituality and peace come as a calming bundle, neatly tied with moments of quiet reflection and deeper understanding. Yet even here, the label might include patience and discipline, as the path to inner peace often requires commitment and letting go of old habits or beliefs.

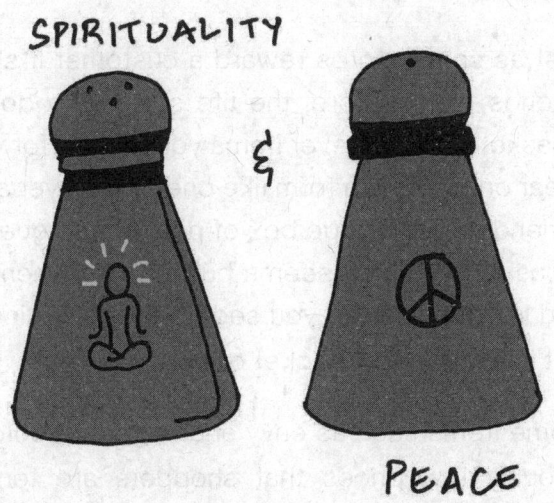

Each bundle in the store tells its own story, and she must weigh the trade-offs carefully, deciding which combinations will truly enrich her life and align with her values.

Just like in a retail store, each customer's basket is different from that of her neighbour's.

In the store of life, given that she has the finite resource—time—she uses items that maximise her contentment. When she gets home, she gets to use anything that is in her basket, and her basket alone. If she spends all her time comparing her basket with that of her fellow shopper's, items such as peace and health will fall from her basket, and in their place, will sit a large box of unhappiness.

I hope that is not you.

Just as some stores reward a customer if she refers her friends to the store, the life store also doubles up your basket with whatever items you wished for your near and dear ones. Fill in a form like one of a prayer asking for your friend to get a large box of peace. And guess what? Your basket suddenly seems bulkier than when you first walked in. And what do you see? Sitting snug inside your basket is a shiny new packet of peace.

Some items such as envy and anger are sold at such ridiculously low prices that shoppers are tempted to hoard them. And before you know it, the basket is filled with only those and the shopper has no place for anything else. Free items do not come cheap, they usually come at a very heavy price.

ANGER & ENVY

Do you spot envy sitting on the shelf with an enticingly low-price tag, practically shouting, "Take me! Everyone else already has"? It is so easy to toss a few packets into the basket without thinking.

Similarly, anger is stocked in bulk, ready to be grabbed at the slightest provocation, and it feels almost free to indulge in. But once these items pile up, they leave no room for kindness, patience or joy. Remember, anger is one letter away from danger.

And what is the price you pay for selecting these?

Envy will slowly drain contentment, making the shopper dissatisfied with her own choices, while anger festers, leaving her exhausted and bitter. What seemed cheap at first glance demands a heavy toll over time, robbing her of peace and meaningful connections.

Free items, after all, rarely come without strings—their hidden price often being paid in the currency of well-being and happiness.

So, what does your basket of life look like and what items are you adding to it? Are they maximising your fulfilment? Maybe it is time to take a good look inside.

🛒 Checkout Counter

1. What are the things that you truly care about?

    a.

    b.

    c.

    d.

    e.

2. What are the things you spend time on that you want to remove from your basket?

    a.

    b.

    c.

2
Think in esreveR

Do you know what you want?

Still thinking?

Although the first principle of getting what you want is *knowing* what you want, sometimes, knowing what you

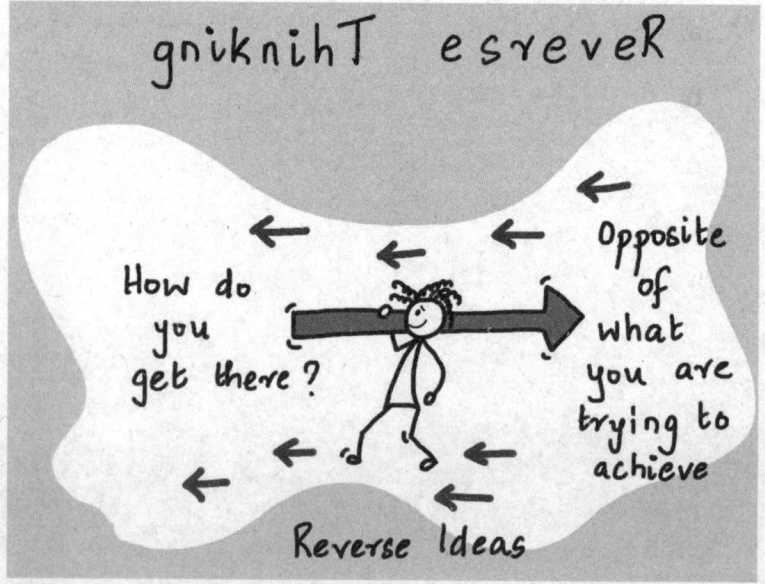

don't want is easier than knowing what you do want. If you are finding it hard to determine the exact "items" that are dear to you and that you want added to your basket so that you can prioritise your time and energy towards those items, you may want to try the technique of thinking in reverse to get to your ideal basket.

Thinking in reverse is a type of brainstorming technique where you identify ways in which you could worsen a problem. Yes, you read this right! You start by stating your problem in reverse, or by changing a positive statement into a negative one, and then tracing the steps needed to address the problem. This technique is great at changing your perspective and helping you look at a problem or situation from a completely new perspective.

For instance, if you are an e-retailer and are trying to increase your customer base, you could try and find a solution by thinking along these lines, "How do I reduce my customer base to zero?"

The question may have many possible answers such as poor user experience of the site, non-competitive pricing, not having enough product selection, too many barriers to adding to cart, bad after-sales experience and so on. You then look at each of these possible scenarios and try to mitigate the risks or fix the issues.

So how do you apply this technique to your basket of life?

What are the things that make you feel discontented or unhappy?

What are the steps you need to take to have them added to your basket of life?

Once you answer these questions, you will easily identify what it is that you do not want to have in your basket and the actions that may lead you to having a sub-optimal one.

Then reverse these to get to your ideal basket content.

Simple!

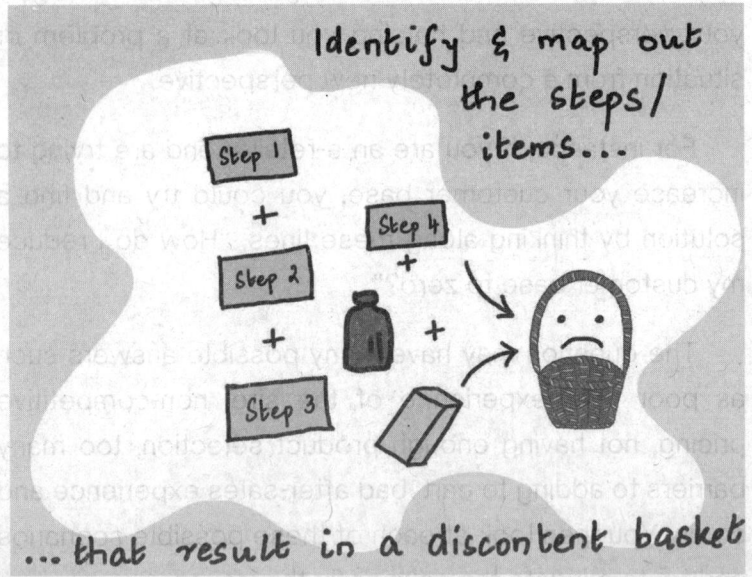

Here are a few examples to get you started on the reverse thinking process.

Being lonely

"Loneliness and the feeling of being unwanted is the most terrible poverty."—Mother Teresa

Scared of being lonely? Now what could be the possible steps you could take in your life to increase your loneliness?

One possible step could be not giving sufficient time to connect with your friends and family. Or letting your ego come in between relationships that matter. Or not giving people your attention when you meet them.

Once you have identified these steps, you reverse them to ensure that this "item" is not added to your

basket of life. So, ensure you give time and attention to people who matter and nurture relationships. Keep your ego in place and check that it is not coming in the way of developing and maintaining a relationship. It may help to be mindful of your pattern of behaviours and make a note of them, so you can become aware of the habit and be more intentional in your behaviour with others.

Being financially dependent

"Your economic security does not lie in your job; it lies in your own power to produce, to think, to learn, to create, to adapt. That's true financial independence. It's not having wealth; it's having the power to produce wealth."— Stephen Covey

Don't want to be financially dependent? What do you think will enable that?

Perhaps splurging on things and living beyond your means? Is it not keeping some money away as savings? Is it not investing your money in instruments that will take care of inflation and help your money grow?

The chapter on habits elucidates the power that small but consistent habits can have on your life, so that maybe you want to take a deeper look at your regular habits to see what needs to be changed to ensure that this item does not get added to your basket, if you believe it is not something you desire.

Being unhealthy

"Whenever I feel the need to exercise, I lie down until it goes away." — Paul Terry

Can't stop eating junk food? Not getting enough exercise? Living a sedentary life? Not getting enough sunlight or sleep?

Want to be healthy and fit?

Well, give up all of the above, and make a lifestyle change to remove the "item" from your basket.

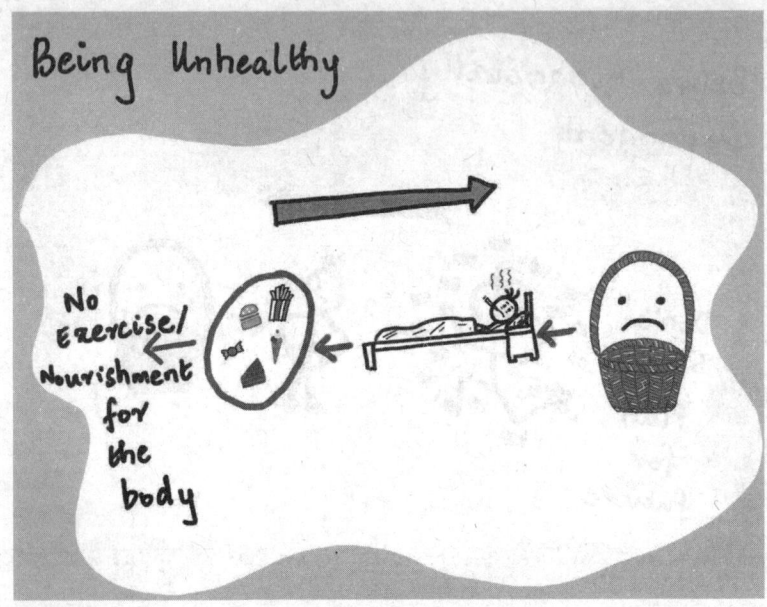

Leaving no legacy behind

"Please think about your legacy because you are writing it every day."—Gary Vaynerchuk.

Living a life without purpose will surely ensure you don't leave a legacy behind.

A legacy can take many forms.

Picasso's legacy is his art, Jane Austen's legacy is her novels, Mozart's legacy is his compositions and Raghu Rai's legacy will be his collection of photographs that capture moments in time. Or perhaps it is a contribution to science or knowledge, like theories, inventions or discoveries that shape the world. From Newton's laws to Marie Curie's groundbreaking work, these legacies endure, influencing generations of thought and progress.

If leaving a legacy is an essential item in your life basket, it is worth considering what you can do now to ensure it is there. These creations hold a piece of your soul and have the power to inspire, move and connect with people long after you are gone. No, you don't have to be a Picasso or Newton to leave a legacy.

A legacy could also be the wisdom you pass on through teaching, mentoring or storytelling, creating ripples that extend far beyond your immediate circle. The people you inspire might carry forward your lessons, building on them in their own unique ways. Sometimes, a legacy isn't about grand gestures but about small, consistent acts of kindness—a word of encouragement, a helping hand or a moment of empathy that leaves a lasting impact in ways you may never fully see.

When was the last time you were kind to a stranger?

Still thinking about how to leave a legacy?

Well, here are a few things that I can suggest:

- Avoid the trap of always prioritising urgent distractions over meaningful pursuits.
- Carve out time for your passion, invest in learning and focus on activities that nourish your soul.

As Vaynerchuk rightly observed—a legacy isn't built in a single moment, but every step you take today helps lay the foundation for something that will stand the test of time. Ready for it?

Sometimes, knowing what is truly important to you may be harder than you think. Thinking in reverse is a good way to distil your thoughts and help you understand what you do not want in your life, so that what you want gets added in your basket.

🛒 Checkout Counter

1. Think about a situation that you've been stuck with for a long time. Will thinking in reverse help with that problem?

2. Think about the "items" you do not want in your basket. List them out here:

   a.

   b.

   c.

3. Identify the steps needed to get those in your basket and check to see if you do some of them subconsciously. Make a note of them so that you can reverse the behaviour.

   a.

   b.

   c.

3

Enjoy the Many Flavours of Saying N

"'No' is a complete sentence."— Anne Lamott

One of the ways to maximise the items you can add to your basket of life and make sure you have the right items in it is about saying yes to the things that make you truly happy.

You can't say yes to everything unless you learn to say no to some other things.

Think of a "No parking" sign or "No smoking" sign or "No pets allowed" sign. What is common among them?

The consistent use of red for "No". Ever wondered why?

The colour red has long been associated with danger, urgency and prohibition, making it a powerful tool to draw attention to things that should be avoided. The consistent use of red for "no" in these contexts has conditioned our minds to associate the colour with negativity, danger and something inherently undesirable.

This subconscious association trickles into our personal lives, making us hesitant to say "no" even when it is the most appropriate response. We begin to view "no" as a negative act, fearing it might upset others, close doors or create conflict. As a result, we avoid it and often end up saying "yes" to things that don't align with our priorities, energy or well-being.

STOP doing that right away!

You are paying a heavy price.

The act of saying no is the green signal to a lot of positive things in life. When you say "no", you are safeguarding your time, energy and mental clarity for what aligns with your values.

Don't want to attend an unnecessary meeting?

Say the magic word "no" and you will find a window of opportunity to work on your passion project.

Don't want to attend a party?

Decline the invitation and create space for rest.

Saying no can be the ultimate self-care.

Saying "NO" creates space for saying "YES"

By filling our lives with unintentional "yes" responses, we leave no room for the opportunities, commitments and passions that truly deserve our attention. Saying "no" is not about rejection or negativity—it is about creating space to say "yes" to the right things. It is a tool for balance, allowing us to focus on what genuinely matters.

"No" becomes a gateway to a meaningful "yes", shifting its connotation from restriction to empowerment.

In the sweltering heat of summers, nothing soothes the mind and body like an ice cream. After all, it is always ice cream o'clock somewhere.

Instead of discussing the many delectable flavours of ice cream, I am going to talk about the many flavours of saying no.

Imagine the word "no" in green as you explore these ideas, consciously working to reframe the colour and associate it with positivity and empowerment.

There are some common scenarios when one would tend to say no. Let us look at the flavour of No-Cream that would work best in each situation.

The Time-Crunch flavour

The first flavour of saying no, which looks like a Choco Chip ice cream and makes me want to have one, is called the Time-Crunch flavour. There are moments in life when we grapple with too many things at the same time and simply do not have the time to do anything more.

When someone asks you to do something that perhaps you are excited about but just do not have the time to do, you pull this delicious-looking No-Cream, take a tasty bite and say, "I'm sorry, but I just don't have the time to do this at the moment."

Do not stop there though.

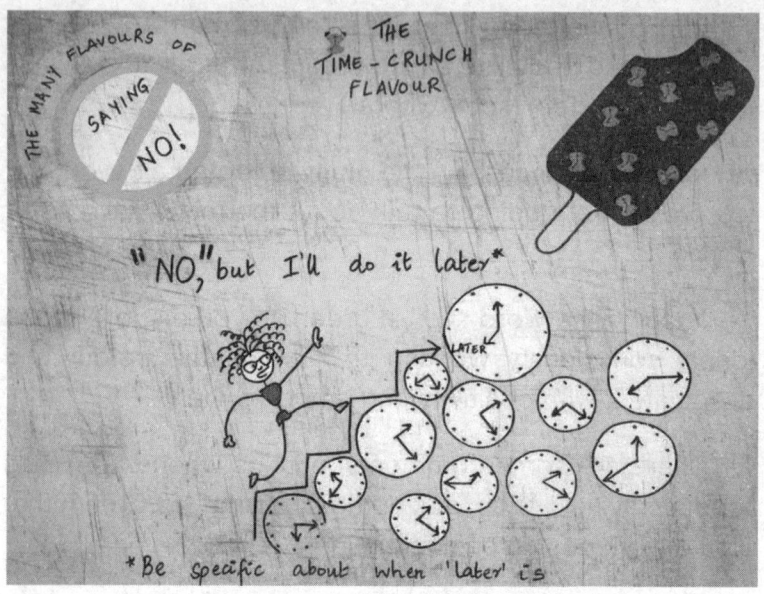

Follow that through with when you think you will be able to get to the task. You show your intention of wanting to perform the task, are unequivocal about not having the time for it, but are specific about when you are likely to be able to have the time.

A senior leader in my organisation used to be very good at using the Time-Crunch flavour. When she was unable to work on something immediately, she would give the person concerned a specific date and time she would get back to the request, immediately add a reminder in her calendar and made sure she followed up on the request at the promised time. This way, she built credibility and trust over a period of time, always responding within the time she had promised and hence could say no with a lot more confidence as time passed.

The Smart-Cookie flavour

One of the trickiest asks which makes people very uncomfortable with saying no is when they are clearly not the subject matter experts in the area, but do not want to be seen as incompetent or less intelligent. They either end up spending a lot of time getting the answer that someone else could have got easily or end up doing a suboptimal job of the ask. A well-timed "no" can save you from unnecessary stress. As Steve Jobs rightly said, "Focus is about saying no."

For situations such as this, savour the Smart-Cookie ice cream and say, "Sorry, but I am not the subject matter expert in this area and hence cannot work on this ask."

But how does one mitigate the risk associated with saying no?

You could suggest someone who may be able to help with the task and offer to connect them with the right person.

In addition to getting the task completed faster and in a more accurate manner, you have also worked towards improving collaboration and connections across people.

Malcolm Gladwell, in his bestselling book *The Tipping Point* describes three kinds of influencers—the Mavens, the Connectors and the Salesmen. The Connectors are people who know everybody; they network in large social circles and are the social glue. You can imagine a Connector naturally loving the Smart-Cookie flavour of saying no, can't you?

Worried about not being a connector?

Don't stress.

You could point them to someone who is, and the odds of them knowing the right person may be so much higher!

Because saying no is not a rejection, it is a redirection.

The Berry-Large Pie flavour

The Berry-Large Pie can be savoured when someone asks you to do too much, and you are unable to do it at all at that given point in time. You could say, "No, I am afraid I cannot do so much." As with all the other No-Cream flavours, follow that statement by volunteering what else you could do instead; in this case, quantifying how much you can do.

Unable to articulate what you can and cannot do?

Ask the person to elaborate. It may help them articulate the ask better to someone else by giving them a smaller and well-defined portion of the task.

Saying no is not about rejection, it is about prioritisation.

Let's say, your housing society wants to run a vaccination camp for the residents of your locality, and they reach out to your mother who is a doctor and ask her if she could run the entire camp. She could respond saying she would be able to help with procuring the vaccines and getting nurses to come on the day, but the co-ordination among the residents, scheduling the slots for each and managing of funds must be picked up by someone else.

Saying no is not about being selfish; it is about being self-aware.

The Not-Cross Bun flavour

The Not-Cross Bun flavour is a powerful and decisive one. It can be relished when someone asks you to do something that makes you cross a personal boundary. This is the only flavour of No-Cream that does not come with a follow-through statement involving any specifics mitigating the perceived negative side effects your no may generate in the person asking for something.

If somebody asks you to do something that makes you uncomfortable and that involves breaking your personal boundary, you respond with a firm, unambiguous, unequivocal NO. There is no "maybe", or "but later" or "perhaps some part of it" in the flavour. It is up to you whether you want to explicitly mention it, as it involves breaking a personal boundary, or let the firmness in your body language convey the message.

Imagine a friend invites you to a party, but you know it will involve a situation that will make you uncomfortable— perhaps the gathering will have people who make inappropriate comments, or you're being asked to engage in activities that don't align with your values. In this case, you would use the Not-Cross Bun flavour. It is as flavoursome as a hot cross bun.

Your response is simple, clear and firm, "No, I won't be attending."

There are no excuses like "Maybe I'll stop by later" or "I'll see if I feel up to it". You don't need to justify it further or explain that you're uncomfortable with the people or the activities. Your boundary is set, and your "no" is enough. Because saying no is the best form of self-respect.

When you relish some of these No-Cream flavours, you automatically create energy, space and time to say yes to things you truly want to do; things that enrich your life basket and help you evolve as a person.

Which flavour do you think you will pick today? You can pick any one of the flavours listed in this chapter or invent a new flavour to suit your needs.

Checkout Counter

1. What are the activities you want to say NO to?

    a.

    b.

    c.

4
Sow the Seeds of Learning

"I have no special talent. I am only passionately curious."
—Albert Einstein

Look where that landed him!

How do you enrich your basket of life? How do you choose activities that bring true contentment and joy?

The masters of contentment, aside from spiritual practitioners and animals, are children.

You may ask why.

Observe them and you will discover two traits that stand out—they live in the present and they are endlessly curious.

As we grow older, our curiosity and our sense of wonder of the world around us seem to diminish.

When was the last time you learned something new?

Learn something New

When was the last time you went deeper into something you already knew a little about?

Learn something deeply

When was the last time you set aside time for learning?

Carol Dweck, in her article on "Growth Mindset", talks about individuals who believe their talents can be developed (through hard work, good strategy and input from others) as having a growth mindset. People with a growth mindset tend to achieve more than those with a fixed mindset because they tend to worry less about looking smart and instead put more energy into, can you guess what? Learning!

The first step to learning something new is to be curious. Why does a natural phenomenon occur? What does cryptography mean? How will the metaverse look like ten years from now? When will the icebergs start melting?

Do questions like these run through your mind?

Being curious helps us to not only discover things about our universe but also helps us understand ourselves better. It expands our thinking and helps us be more empathetic towards people and situations that are unlike ours. Develop a passion for learning and you will never stop to grow.

MAKE TIME FOR LEARNING

So how do you go about being curious and make learning part of your DNA if it does not come naturally? It all starts with making learning a priority and taking time out for it. As the Chinese proverb goes, Learning is a treasure that follows its owner everywhere.

Easier said than done? No, it is quite easy to sow the seeds of learning.

Here are seven ways in which you can make time for learning:

Set up time on your calendar

"Knowledge has to be improved, challenged and increased constantly, or it vanishes." —Peter Drucker

Choose a time slot that you will dedicate towards learning and block it on your calendar. I have seen that keeping it at the same time each day makes it easier to follow. The intent, the energy and the focus fall into place more naturally when you do it at the same hour. Blocking time on the calendar also means nothing else can take your attention away from your time of learning.

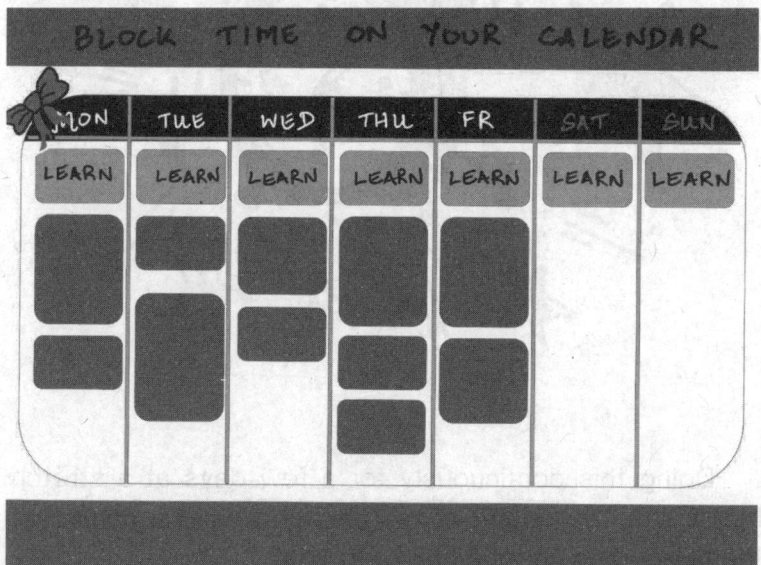

Keep an alarm

This tip involves keeping an alarm on your phone to stop you from whatever else you are doing and to get started on learning. Often times, a loud shrill sound breaks the thinking pattern and jolts us out of our mind into the present. That pause in thinking is a good way to refocus the mind on what we deem important for us.

Doing this continuously for a few days at a stretch helps sow the seeds of learning and build a habit that then becomes second nature to you.

Get a friend or a family member to remind you

This tip relies on the human factor.

Share your goal with either a family member or a friend. Ask them to hold you accountable to your decision. With this, you have "escalated" your resolution from just making one for yourself to sharing it with someone else. The act of sharing your goal with someone helps keep a check on your progress and keep you on the track to learning because the opinion of a close one matters.

Setting yourself a goal like wanting to learn something new every year or every few years and sharing that with someone else will make you find something to learn, lest they ask you about it in the future.

While the idea of wanting to learn something new each year makes it easier to track, often it does not give you enough time to delve deep into the subject. Increasing the time period between learning new things helps you delve deeper into a subject. When you are doing that, however, make sure to have goals that are measurable so that you can track your progress along your journey.

"You can't wait for inspiration, you have to go after it with a club."—Jack London

Choose a day of the week that is reserved for learning

A key element of Google's innovative culture in the early 2000s was the "20% Time" policy, which allowed employees to dedicate 20 per cent of their work time to projects they were passionate about. The founders believed it empowered their employees to be more creative and innovative and led to significant advances to their products. Google gifted their employees time to learn and to innovate.

Guess what were the outcomes?

This policy resulted in the development of groundbreaking products such as Gmail, Google News and AdSense, significantly enhancing Google's product portfolio and employee motivation.

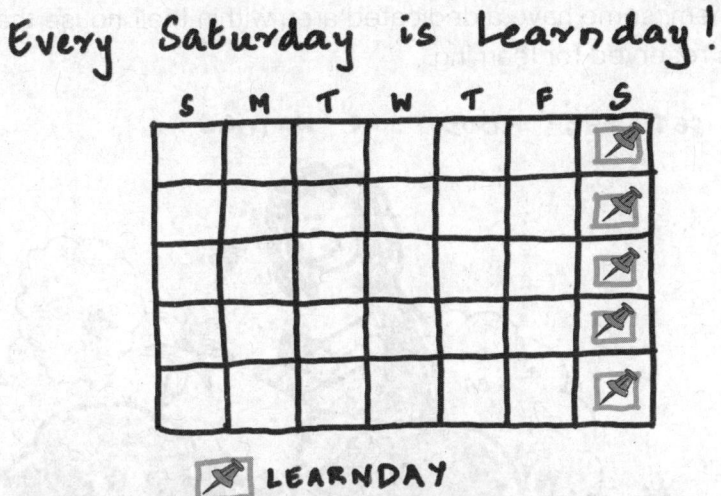

Borrowing from Google's idea, you may want to choose a day of the week that is dedicated to learning too. Choose to learn either something new or go deeper into something you already know a little of. By practising this continuously over a period of time, you make sowing the seeds of learning a habit.

Set the mood

Having a dedicated space for learning automatically sends a message to the brain when you enter that space, and your energies are then aligned to learning. Different people like different kinds of spaces for learning: some like it out in the open close to nature; some like to be in the middle of the hustle and bustle of an active area; some like to be in a quiet space with nothing to disturb them; some have a dedicated area within their house that is reserved for learning.

SET THE MOOD : IN NATURE

SET THE MOOD : IN THE MIDST OF CHAOS

SET THE MOOD : IN SILENCE

Explore what kinds of spaces work best for you and choose an area that is meant just for learning. If you repeatedly go into that space and do some learning, after a period, your mind automatically switches into learning mode the moment you step into that area.

Studies have also shown music to be a potential factor for improving the process of learning and knowledge retention. In the 1960s, Dr Georgi Lozanov and Evelyna Gateva revolutionised the teaching methodology by introducing a learning method called Accelerated Learning by using background music to help students learn and assimilate the learning. Music often places people in the relaxed alpha brain wave state, thus helping them stabilise their mental and physical rhythms and enabling them to absorb their learning.

SET THE MOOD: MUSIC

Talking about music is like dancing about architecture. Go switch on the music and tap into an inspiration!

Get physical

By exercising regularly, you boost the release of happy hormones in your body.

Yes, you read that right. So, stop groaning and start exercising.

Numerous studies have shown that engaging in physical activity releases endorphin and serotonin that enhance your mood and trigger a positive feeling in the body. And what better way to learn something new and absorb the learning than by putting yourself in a happy mental space?

I have felt my mind to be most alert and refreshed soon after I exercise. It helps me get fresh perspectives and puts me in a state where I am open to new experiences. It leaves no room for the feeling "stuck in the rut".

Try exercising for at least thirty minutes and watch how it activates your mind and lets you get in the "zone".

Absorb the learning

"Immediately the old grey house upon the street rose up like a stage set ... the house, the town, the square where I was sent before lunch, the streets along which I used to run errands, the country roads we took ... in that moment ... the whole of Combray and of its surroundings ... sprang into being, town and gardens alike, all from my cup of tea."

In *Remembrance of Things Past*, Marcel Proust famously describes his sensory déjà vu, which he experienced after tasting the tea-soaked crumbs of a madeleine. Just one taste of the sweet, buttery French cake mingled with lime-blossom tea was all it took for childhood memories to come flooding back.

Whether it is a tea-soaked madeleine, your grandmother's samosa or your mother's perfume, a "Proustian moment" is when a particular scent conjures up a certain experience, time or a place.

There is a proven link between taste buds and memories.

"When nothing else subsists from the past, after the people are dead, after the things are broken and scattered ... the smell and taste of things remain poised a long time, like souls ... bearing resiliently on tiny and almost impalpable drops of their essence, the immense edifice of memory."— Marcel Proust

Taste to Memory Linkage

From an evolutionary point of view, one of the most important forms of memory is taste recognition memory.

The link between taste buds and memories originally came about as a survival tactic known as conditioned taste aversion, which is the learned association between the taste of a particular food and the illness it may cause.

Whenever you need to remember facts, try reading the facts while eating something. When you want to regurgitate the facts, try eating the same food to bring back the memory of learning those facts. In addition to the food being absorbed by the body, let some learning be absorbed by it too!

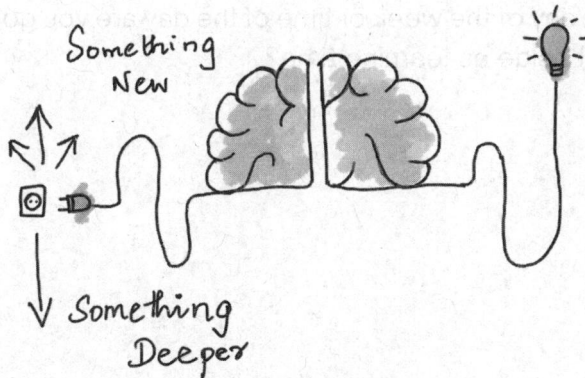

So, what are you going to learn today or this week? And what are you going to use to help you stick to your plan and build a habit of learning?

🛒 Checkout Counter

1. What new things do you want to learn?

    a.

    b.

    c.

2. What are the things you want to spend more time in learning?

    a.

    b.

    c.

3. What day of the week or time of the day are you going to set aside as learning time?

5

The Compounding Effect of Habits

"Watch your actions; they become habits. Watch your habits; they become your character. Watch your character; they become your destiny."—The Buddha

Any "item" you want in your basket of life needs consistent care and nurturing to become a significant part of your life. It is your daily habits that shape your traits, and those traits, in turn, grow into the priorities that define what truly matters to you.

Habits are like insurance—you invest in them when everything seems fine, so that you can bank on them when you need them most. Built from small, consistent actions carried out over time, habits have the power to transform your aspirations into reality, creating a foundation for long-term growth and success.

Here is a simple yet powerful example to illustrate the impact of small, consistent habits over time. Imagine starting with your face turned to the right. Now, slowly begin turning it towards the left—so gradually that someone watching wouldn't notice any difference.

With each tiny adjustment, it seems as though nothing has really changed. But after some time, the transformation becomes undeniable—your face is now fully turned to the left!

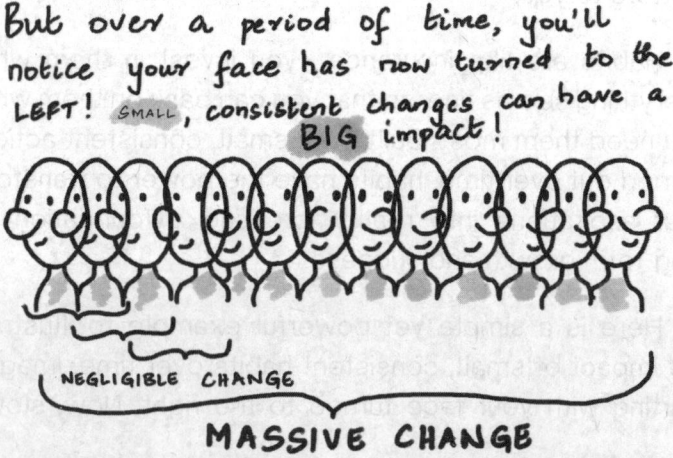

Small, consistent actions may seem insignificant initially, but over time, they create profound, lasting change. They can also lead to a complete 180-degree shift in your perspective, allowing you to see the world—and yourself—in an entirely new light.

Saving money

I am sure you are familiar with the concept of the compounding effect when it comes to saving money. The principle is simple: as your savings earn interest, that interest is added to your principal amount, and in turn, this larger sum generates even more interest. Over a long period, this snowball effect can transform modest savings into a significant financial cushion.

Now, who wouldn't want to lay their head on such a cushion?

You must be wondering money can't buy happiness. But poverty can't buy anything.

For example, consider a small amount saved consistently each month. Initially, the growth might seem slow and almost negligible. But as the years go by, the power of compounding accelerates, and your savings can grow into a substantial sum. This accumulated wealth can eventually provide you with the financial freedom to live in peace, even when other streams of income may no longer be available.

The process is quite simple actually:

1. Make money.
2. Use that money to make more money.
3. REPEAT.

As someone wise once told me, "Making money is an action, keeping money is behaviour and growing money is knowledge."

The compounding effect is a testament to patience and consistency, showing how small, steady efforts can yield enormous benefits in the long run—not just financially but in other areas of life as well.

Exercising

Let's say, you invest in exercise for a few minutes in a day, and keep at that habit for a long period of time. On the first day, you may not see any visible benefit from the habit; in fact, it may be painful to be spending time on exercise when you could have been pursuing a dozen other pleasure-seeking activities. But, if you start with just fifteen minutes a day rather than an hour, for example, you might not mind it as much. It is usually easier to keep it going regularly because it will not feel like a big "sacrifice", and it is finished soon enough!

A month later, on one Saturday afternoon, you may realise you have not been feeling drowsy like you had all the previous years and have more energy to work on the garden that you have been thinking of tending to for the last six months.

A year after, you may find you have fallen sick far fewer times than you had in the past. The icing on the cake (that you can now relish because of how fit you are) will be when you go for your reunion a decade after you have graduated and notice you look fitter than most of your peers. Those fifteen minutes of exercise over the years will give you what no anti-ageing cream could have ever given you! The precious minutes you invested in exercising that showed no obvious benefit at the beginning, had, over a period, compounded itself into a force to reckon with, and had turned you into a healthier, fitter and more energetic person. When you exercise, you don't sweat, you sparkle.

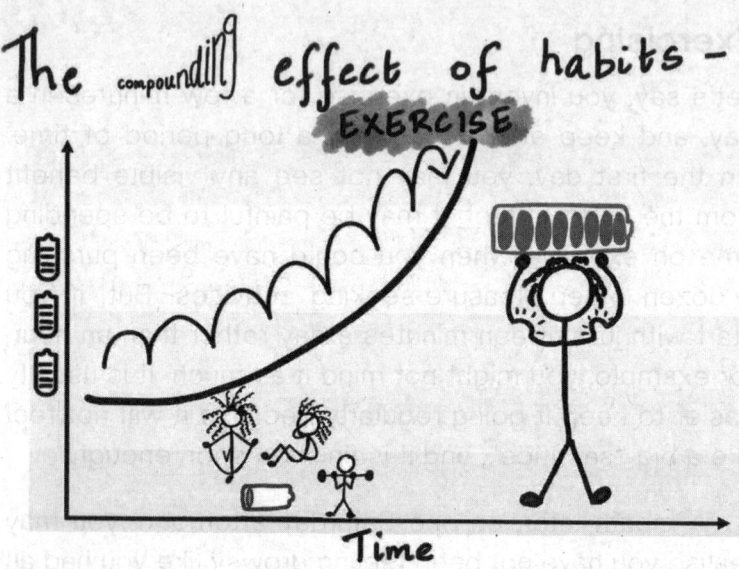

Meditating

"Your mind is your instrument, learn to play it well."—Tamara Levitt

Choose habits you want to prioritise and give them time, depending on what "items" you put into your basket of life. For example, if spirituality and peace are important to you, find something small you can do every day that makes you a more peaceful being. It could be sitting in silence and meditating for a few minutes daily, or chanting a mantra that brings you peace, or lighting a lamp and saying a prayer, or gardening. Choose an activity that appeals to you and block a time during the day for when you will invest in it.

Fellow meditators have often cited how they are more peaceful, balanced and focused, thanks to their practice. Sometimes, you look at a person and sense the positivity emanating from them and tend to attribute it to their personality, but personality is often a result of repetitive habits that they choose to prioritise over others.

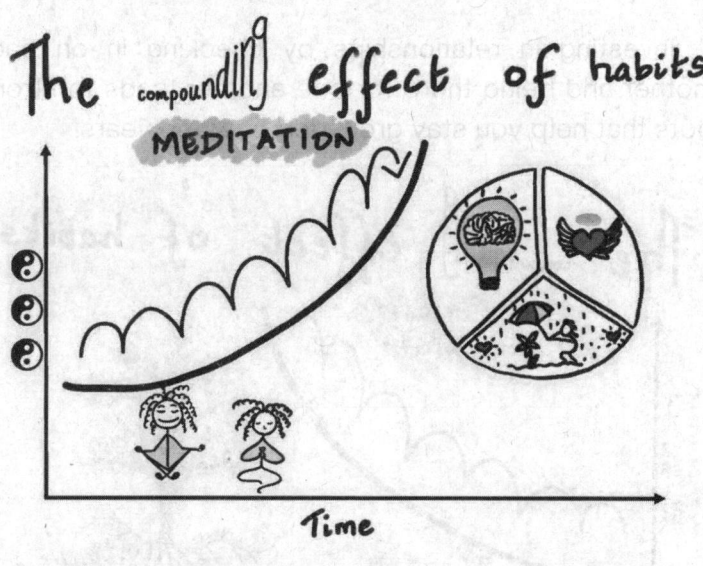

Investing in relationships

"To live is to suffer; to survive is to find some meaning in the suffering."—Friedrich Nietzsche

Just like the Buddha experienced and taught—to live is to suffer, be it due to sickness, poverty, poor health, or the loss of a loved one. While we are not going to delve into the noble eightfold path to liberate ourselves from suffering in this book, studies have shown that the strength of interpersonal relationships almost always is a great predictor of how happy a person is and it helps them deal with adversity in a better manner. As the old Buddhist saying goes, "Pain in inevitable, but suffering is optional."

Investing in relationships by checking in on each another and being there for one another leads to strong roots that help you stay grounded over the years.

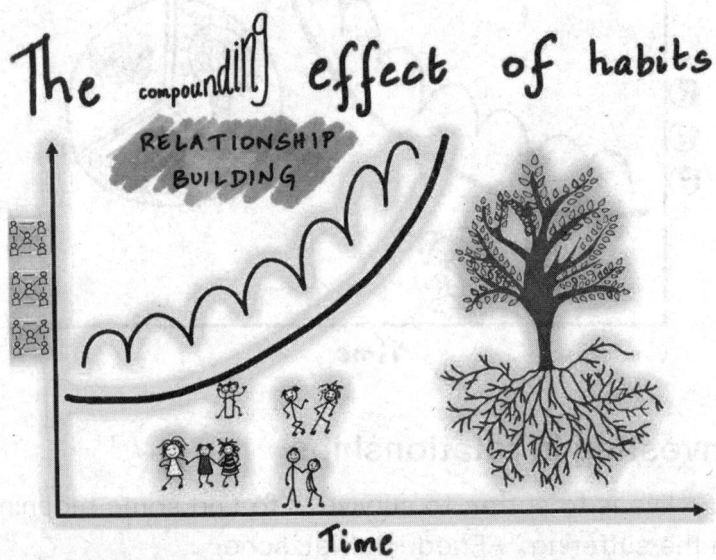

Reading

As the motivational speaker, Jim Rohn, famously said, "You are the average of the five people you spend the most time with." Now imagine if you spent most of your time with books, you could be the average of many great personalities like Isaac Newton, Leonardo da Vinci, Maya Angelou, Steve Jobs and Steffi Graf!

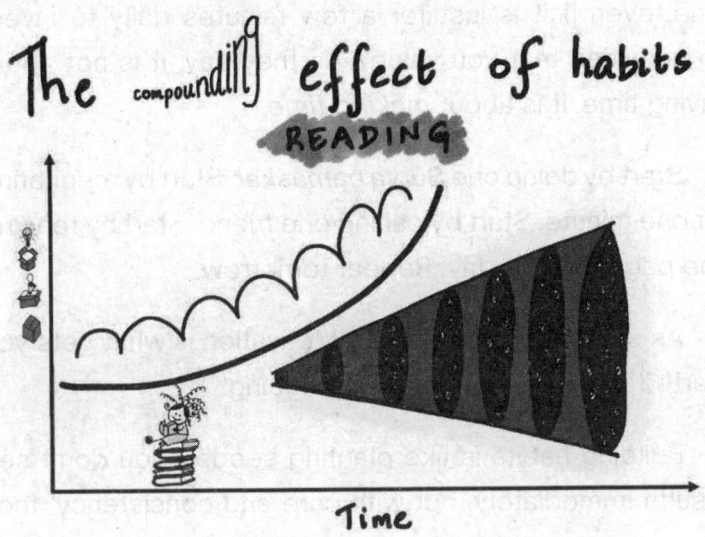

You could be the average of the best scientist, the best philosopher, the best sportsperson, the best businessman and the best painter!

Reading at least a few pages every day makes your universe expand over the years. I once came across a beautiful thought: "Birds have wings. Humans have books."

How true!

Reading is my safest place and my wildest adventure.

Habits people have invested in reflect in the choice of their careers, personality and life. It may be worthwhile to look at how you spend each day of your life and check to see if the minutes you spend on each activity go towards enriching your basket of life. If not, could you free up some time, even if it is just for a few minutes daily to invest on activities that you value? As they say, it is not about having time, it is about *making time.*

Start by doing one *Surya namaskar*. Start by meditating for one minute. Start by calling one friend. Start by reading one page. Start today. Repeat tomorrow.

As someone wisely said, "Motivation is what gets you started. Habit is what keeps you going."

Building habits is like planting seeds—you don't see results immediately, but with care and consistency, they grow into something strong and lasting.

🛒 Checkout Counter

1. What activities are you going to do regularly?

    a.

    b.

    c.

2. How much time will you regularly spend on them?

    a.

    b.

    c.

6

Ask for Help

There are moments in life when you may feel as if there is too much going on; that you cannot possibly handle everything together. This is usually a great time to inspect what you have put in your basket of life and to check to ensure that you have only those things that are truly important to you.

"It's not enough to be busy. The question is, what are we busy about?"—Henry David Thoreau

Keep your basket in mind...

In order to prioritise what to keep, you may want to look at what is important to you and what you can control and keep only those which fall under these categories.

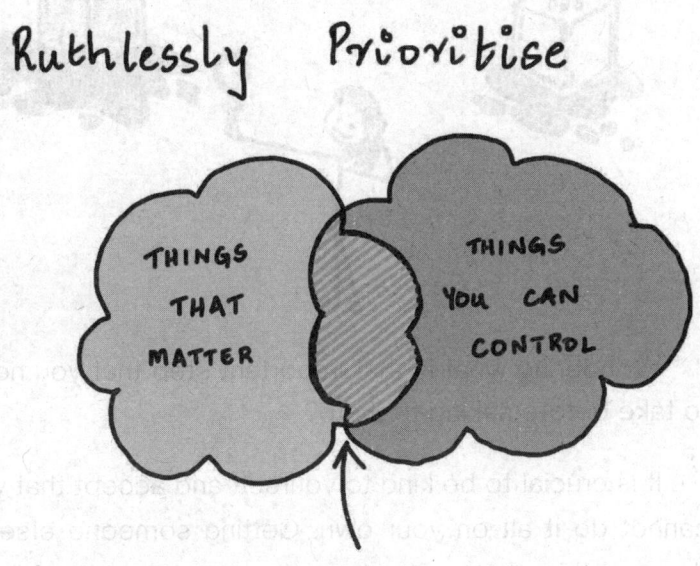

"The key is not to prioritize what's on your schedule, but to schedule your priorities."—Stephen Covey.

Asking for help around items that fall outside of the intersection will go a long way in adding some balance to your basket. There are two key elements you will need to give up when asking for help—your ego and your sense of control.

And it is not easy to give up both, right?

Ask for Help

Wondering what is that important step that you need to take before asking for help?

It is crucial to be kind to yourself and accept that you cannot do it all on your own. Getting someone else to do something automatically means you have to give up some element of control, acknowledging the final output may not be of the same quality as what you may have produced. Don't be shy about asking for help. It does not mean you are weak; it only means you are wise.

Knowing which battles to fight and which to let go of is an essential skill, especially during the demanding phases of life. As a mother, I learned this lesson the hard way, discovering that striving for perfection in everything was a recipe for burnout. There was a time when I believed that the house always needed to be sparkling clean, that every meal had to be hand-cooked and delicious enough to rival a restaurant's offerings. But as the demands of motherhood grew, I realised that holding on to these standards was not only unsustainable, but also unnecessary.

I began by letting go of some of these self-imposed expectations. I passed on certain responsibilities, like asking others in the household to take charge of cleaning or cooking. When I had to be away, I turned to my parents for help in managing my child. The truth is, we wouldn't have managed without their unwavering support. They stepped in with open arms, offering not just help but immense amount of love, patience and wisdom. Their presence lightened our load and strengthened the foundation of our family.

This experience not only enriched their bond with my child but also deepened our relationship with them. It reminded us of how much they had already done for us and how much they continued to give. What began as a call for help blossomed into a stronger, more loving connection—a partnership built on gratitude and mutual care, which remains a source of strength and warmth to this day.

"Pick battles big enough to matter, small enough to win."
—Jonathan Kozol

Choose which (metaphorical) battles to fight

Sometimes, contentment means knowing when to let go of the small battles so that you can focus on winning the war. For me, this "war" was about being present for my child, maintaining my emotional and mental well-being and creating a home filled with love rather than perfection. Whether life demands you to let go of minor irritations or step back from seemingly important tasks, it is this ability to choose your battles that allows you to not only survive but also thrive.

In making the choice around which battles to fight, go back to your basket, prioritise ruthlessly knowing what items are most important to you, let go of some control and don't sweat over small stuff. The outcome of getting someone else to help with something may not meet your standards of quality but put things in perspective and

Don't sweat the small stuff!

let go. Like me, a lot of new mothers grapple with the enormity of managing a baby, a full-time job and running a household. Not sweating the small stuff could be not worrying about having the house completely clean and not worrying about what other people may think of you; getting some help with cooking (may not be as healthy or as nutritious as you would've liked); and getting family to stay with you (may result in a loss of privacy but prioritise). In that current state of life, a new mother may have parenthood and career as the only two items in her basket, and prioritising those two over all else will lead to contentment at that moment.

As Oprah Winfrey rightly observed, "You can have it all. You just can't have it all at once."

🛒 Checkout Counter

1. Is there any area in your life where you feel overwhelmed? Can you explore whether you can ask for help? What can you ask for and whom can you reach out to?

2. What are some areas you are willing to give up control? Can you ask someone to help you with these?

7

Learn to Delete

"Happiness is a place between too little and too much."
— Finnish proverb

Over the past few years, you must have seen a surge in interest in de-cluttering physical spaces to create mental clarity, emotional relief, and more room for joy and happiness. This practice isn't just about tidying up; it is about making intentional choices to let go of what no longer serves you, so that you can focus on what truly enriches your life.

Imagine stepping into a wardrobe crammed with clothes you have not worn in years. The sheer variety of choices makes it harder for you to decide what to wear, often leaving you feeling frustrated about wasting precious time. Decluttering your wardrobe—keeping only the items you love to wear—can go a long way in reducing your agony and allowing you to focus on what is important instead of agonising over choices that do not align with your needs.

Your home is a living space, not a storage space. As the saying goes, "You never have to throw away that which you never buy." Let that guide your choices.

Now, extend this idea beyond physical spaces. Consider a schedule overloaded with tasks that could easily be delegated. Let us say you are trying to juggle work, household chores and personal goals, all at once. By identifying tasks that you can pass on to others—like hiring someone to clean your home or delegating certain work responsibilities to a colleague—you free up mental space to focus on bigger priorities, such as spending quality time with your family or advancing a meaningful project.

Another example is the mental clutter that comes from managing too many commitments. A cluttered mind, filled with unnecessary worries or tasks that don't align with your values, can leave you feeling scattered and drained. By learning to say "no" to unimportant demands and outsourcing where possible, you create room in your mind to focus on what truly matters—whether it is nurturing relationships, pursuing a passion, or simply finding moments of peace.

Even in a kitchen filled with gadgets and tools you rarely use, delegation can play a role. Let go of the idea that you need to cook every meal from scratch, and instead, consider delegating by ordering in occasionally or involving family members in meal prep. Clearing this expectation from your plate not only frees physical space, but also gives you time to savour the moments that truly matter.

Decluttering, whether it is your home, schedule or mental load, isn't just about removing the unnecessary; it is about creating space for what adds value to your life.

If it does not add to your life, it does not belong in your life. By focusing on what is important and letting go of the rest, you allow yourself to live with intention, clarity and joy.

How do you clear your mind?

Noting down what needs to be done removes the need for the mind to remember one additional detail, and lets you focus on the important. You can keep modifying the list every time you remember what needs to be done.

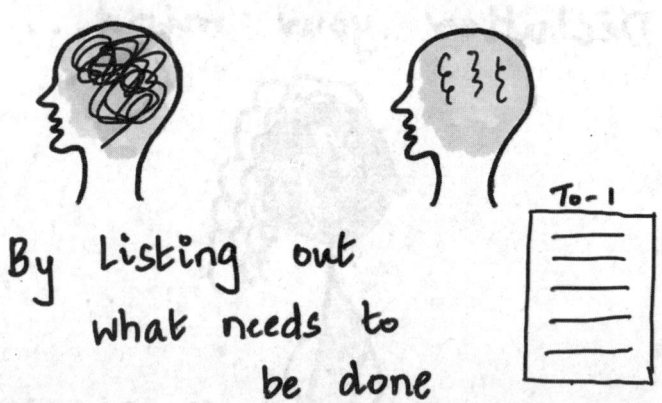

Listing out what needs to be done is just a small part of the solution. The bigger piece is realising that not everything on the list needs to be done by you alone.

Doing it all by yourself

Getting others to Help!

As the popular saying goes, no (wo)man is an island. Asking for help or getting someone else to pitch in, very often results in an end product that is of much higher quality than the one you would have got if you had tried to do it alone.

Things aren't adding up in your life? Start subtracting!

Abra-ca-delegate!

Delegating and asking for help may seem similar, but they serve different purposes and involve distinct dynamics. Delegation is about assigning responsibility for a task to someone else, often with clear authority and autonomy to carry it out. It is a proactive, structured process where you entrust someone with a job that aligns with their skills or role. For example, delegating a project to a team member at work involves handing over not just the task, but also the decision-making authority within defined boundaries.

Asking for help, on the other hand, is a reactive process that occurs when you recognise you need assistance to complete something you cannot manage alone. Help often comes with a shared responsibility where the person assisting you might not have full ownership of the task. For instance, asking a friend to help you move house doesn't mean they take over the planning or execution entirely—they assist you with specific aspects.

In essence, delegation empowers others by giving them ownership, while asking for help involves shared effort and often emotional support. Both are valuable tools for optimising outcomes and achieving balance, but understanding their distinction allows you to use them effectively in different scenarios.

Delegate to maintain balance

Delegating or asking for help is not just limited to the workplace; it is equally, if not more, important at home.

What is the first step that you take in this direction?

Recognise that you can't do everything on your own.

Step 2?

Identify the areas where you need assistance.

Let us dig deeper.

Track your activities for a few days to pinpoint where most of your time goes and which tasks can be handed over. Can you outsource your routine chores like doing the laundry, grocery shopping or prepping meals? These are tasks where the outcome does not significantly impact your life, but freeing up that time can make a big difference.

Can you ask your friend or a trusted family member to help your child with their schoolwork or plan a family event?

When asking for their support, be clear about what you need and offer to return the favour when possible.

You might be surprised by how willingly people step in if you simply ask.

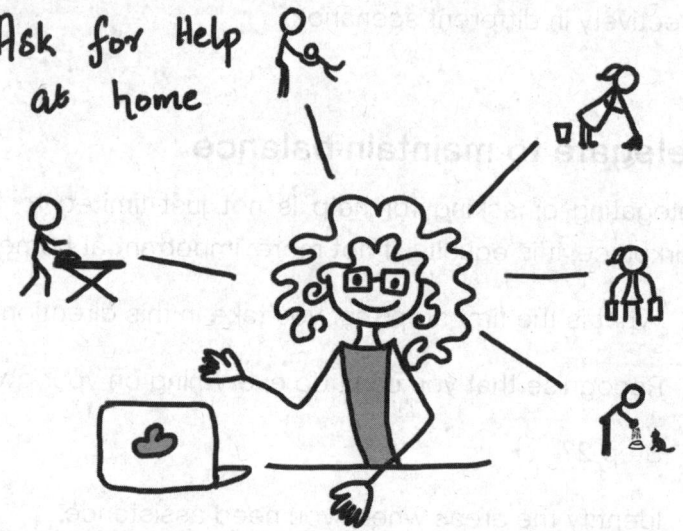

Ultimately, deciding what not to do is as important as deciding what to do. Reclaim your time and energy to invest in what truly matters to you because fostering balance and reducing unnecessary stress are critical.

Delegate to focus on the important

Are you the sort of person whose to-do list has sub-lists that are categorised by genre, deadline, priority, geography and feelings?

Do they run into pages and pages with some items crossed off and some items that continue to live on the list eternally?

If either of these scenarios is your truth, you may be trying to do too much, all by yourself, without delegating to others.

Let us say you have a family reunion coming up. Feeling overwhelmed?

It is natural. Don't stress. Relax.

What is on top of the priority list? Spending quality time with loved ones, right?

How do you go about achieving this?

Delegate. DELEGATE. Delegate.

How?

You may assign the task of booking the venue to one sibling, planning the menu to another and coordinating logistics like transportation or lodging of guests to a trusted cousin.

Instead of carrying the burden of managing every detail, focus on adding personal touches like writing heartfelt invitations, preparing a family slideshow or organising a group activity that brings everyone together.

Clearly communicating your expectations and trusting your family members to handle their assigned responsibilities ensures the event comes together seamlessly.

Ensure everyone contributes to the shared goal of a joyful gathering.

By delegating these tasks, you didn't just lighten your load, but also gave yourself the opportunity to connect better with your loved ones and direct your energy to parts of the experience that mean the most to you.

Delegate to let others grow

Do you find yourself wishing that someone—anyone—would take over the dishes? And does that "someone" often include your teenage offspring? Well, that is just the beginning!

Why stop at dishes when you can take it to the next level?

How about teaching your teenager at home how to cook? This is especially lifesaving if your teenage kid keeps going around uttering WTF (Where's the Food?) all day. You might typically handle all the cooking, but by delegating this task to them, you provide an opportunity for them to grow and learn. Start with something simple like making a dosa or baking cookies. Walk them through the process the first time, then step back and let them try on their own.

Not only does this take one task off your plate, but it also energises them by giving them a sense of responsibility and accomplishment. Who knows? Over time, they may develop a passion for cooking and even surprise you with a gourmet dinner one day. Delegating responsibilities at home fosters collaboration and creates moments of shared joy and learning at home.

Thus, delegation could end up as a blessing in disguise. By delegating you equip others with new skills and greater confidence.

Delegate to get the best person on the job

Imagine organising a Ganesh Chaturthi celebration in your residential society. Different members of the community bring unique skills and strengths to the table, and assigning tasks based on these ensures the event is seamless and enjoyable for everyone.

Do you have an artistically inclined neighbour? Perhaps they could take the task of decorating the pandal with beautiful garlands, rangoli and lights.

The foodie in the group might take charge of organising the prasad preparation or coordinating a feast.

Someone who is well-connected in the local area could manage the logistics—arranging the Ganesh idol, sourcing materials for the puja and coordinating with vendors.

A tech-savvy member could handle sending out digital invites and live-streaming the festivities for those who can't attend in person.

By tapping into these strengths of others, everyone feels a deep sense of involvement and pride in their contributions whether it is the decoration that is appreciated, or the prasad, or the smooth execution of the event.

Since festivals are often a community affair, recognising and leveraging individual strengths isn't just practical—it is a celebration of the diversity and talent within the community, creating shared memories and fostering a deeper sense of togetherness.

You don't have to do everything! Even Batman had Robin.

I have a simple plan—I either delegate something; I drop it; or I deal with it.

What is *your* plan?

Checkout Counter

1. What activities can someone else do at home? Whom will you ask for help?

    a.

    b.

    c.

2. What activities will you delegate to others at work?

    a.

    b.

    c.

8

Get Things D✓ne

- How many pages does your to-do list run into?
- How many times have you procrastinated on a task and felt miserable about it after?
- How often have you seen someone easily complete multiple tasks with elan and wondered how they did it?

Is "tomorrow" often the busiest day of the week for you? You are not the only one. So how do you break the cycle?

Find ways to overcome the reasons for your procrastination.

Two reasons are attributed to this common phenomenon. People tend to postpone a task or activity because it is either big and scary, or small (unimportant) and boring.

The most important part of the journey in getting things done is identifying which category the postponed activity falls under.

To-Do List

1. Make lists
2. Look at lists
3. PANIC!

The above is certainly not what you should do.

If the task is big and/or scary, the trick is taking the problem head-on and breaking it into smaller tasks.

Take the problem head-on...

... and break it into smaller elements

Once you have broken it down into smaller tasks, you can apply the super useful urgent versus important matrix popularly known as the Eisenhower Matrix to determine what action needs to be taken. No, it is not as scary as it sounds.

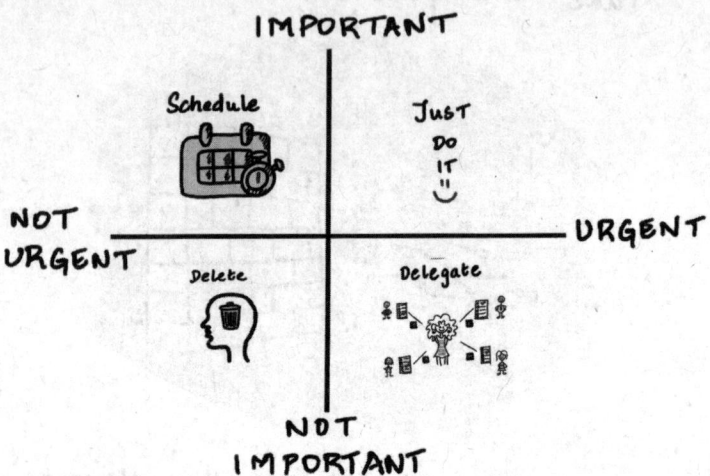

Is there any urgent task to complete?

Will it take you less than five minutes to do it?

Then do it!

Instead of putting it on a to-do list and burdening your mind with that undone task, just do it.

Imagine waking up in the morning, groggy and tempted to leave the bed in disarray as you rush to start your day. It is easy to think, *I'll make my bed later* because you are not lazy, you are simply in an energy-saving mode!

But that mess lingers, greeting you every time you walk in. And worst of all, it robs you of the ultimate reward—*bedgasm*—that pure bliss of sinking into a clean and cosy bed at the end of a long day.

All you have to do is take a couple of minutes to pull up the duvet, straighten the pillows and smooth out the sheets as soon as you get up. It is a small, quick action that immediately creates a sense of order and accomplishment, setting a positive tone for the rest of your day. Unless you thrive in chaos ...

This simple habit gives you a subtle psychological boost—proof that even small wins, like a neatly made bed, can contribute to a more organised and focused mindset.

Ticking one thing off your list, no matter how small, typically tends to energise you and leaves you with a feeling of accomplishment. It also sets the tone for the day, by changing your internal energy to that of getting things done, rather than of putting off tasks for later or feeling lethargic.

If a task takes less than five minutes...

JUST DO IT !!

Often, a task can be broken down into smaller elements, and once you do that most things can be completed fast. Finishing those small tasks rather than listing them all on a list as pending activities can energise you and leave you in a space where you are ready for the tasks which remain.

Let us discuss our favourite task for the year—Diwali cleaning.

Feeling overwhelmed already? Every corner seems to be calling for attention—cupboards overflowing with unused items, shelves layered with dust, and decorative diyas and lights buried somewhere in storage.

Instead of freezing at the enormity of it all, simply break it down into smaller tasks.

First, declutter your wardrobe, setting aside clothes for donation—a quick 30-minute job.

Second, dust the most-used surfaces in the living room.

Finally, retrieve the box of festive decorations and neatly arrange them, ready for the big day.

Are you feeling lighter already? When the monumental task of Diwali cleaning becomes manageable, it leaves your spirit lighter, and you are ready to welcome the festival (and twenty others) with joy and positivity.

Finishing up the 80% can act as an energizer to tackle the hard 20%

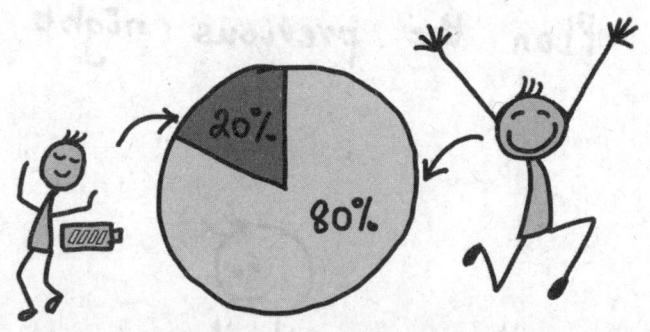

For tasks that fall under the Not Important but Urgent quadrant, it is best to delegate it to someone else. I will not dwell on that matter since there is an entire chapter that deals with delegation along with reasons to delegate and means of delegating.

I will focus the rest of this chapter on activities that fall under the Important but Not Urgent category; the ones that tend to find themselves on to-do lists and the ones that most often remain on that list for a long time causing much grief and anxiety.

What can you do to ease your pain?

Plan the night before

"Before anything else, preparation is the key to success."
—Alexander Graham Bell

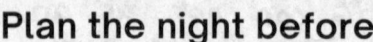

It is very helpful to plan the next day's activities the previous night. There is no need to get into the details but just knowing the four or five things that need to be accomplished the next day gets your mind prepared for what is coming.

Am I stating the obvious? Not really.

You'd be surprised how much anxiety comes not from the task itself, but from the fear or discomfort of not knowing what needs to be done.

Planning helps to bring those into the light of the "known" and calms the mind to actually getting things done.

Let me share how I dealt with it recently.

I had a busy day ahead as it was my daughter's school annual day function. There were costumes to pack, snacks to prepare and last-minute errands to run, and the details felt overwhelming. But I did not let the uncertainty keep me up all night.

Instead of tossing and turning, I took a few minutes to plan the night before. I listed down everything:
- ironing the costume,
- packing a water bottle and snacks,
- charging my phone for photos and
- checking the event timings.

As I jotted these down, the chaos in my mind started to dissipate.

The next morning, instead of scrambling in panic, I calmly ticked off tasks one by one. Having clarity from the night before ensured the day ran smoothly, leaving me relaxed and able to fully enjoy my child's big moment.

Start the day right

Does your day look like this?
1. Get up
2. Survive
3. Go back to bed

Build a world that makes you jump out of bed at 5 a.m. Also, focus on getting a good start to the day. By waking up early and at around the same time each day, your body aligns with its circadian rhythm, the natural internal clock that regulates sleep-wake cycles. This helps optimise energy levels and prepares you for the activities that follow during the day.

Have you noticed how often the morning you have determines how the rest of the day pans out? A crappy start to the day usually extends to the rest of the day. A good start to the day is your best bet at having a great day. Be mindful of how you start your day.

Build some good routines away from technology in the morning.

"You need to remember that your excuses are seducers, your fears are liars and your doubts are thieves."
—Robin Sharma

Apply the Pomodoro Technique

The Pomodoro (tomato in Italian) Technique is a time-blocking technique that involves breaking work into intervals of time, typically 25 minutes long.

The Pomodoro Technique

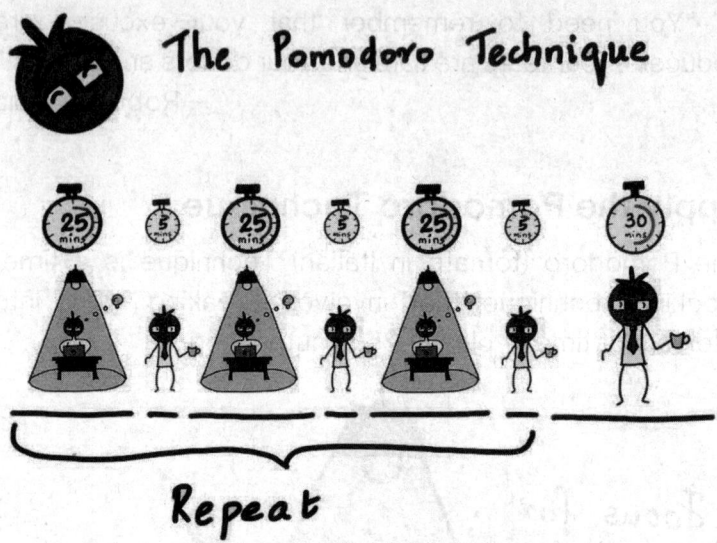

At the end of the 25 minutes of focused time, take a short break of five minutes to recuperate.

This popular time management method asks you to alternate pomodoros, that is, focused work sessions with frequent short breaks to promote sustained concentration and stave off mental fatigue.

After every four pomodoros, take a longer break of about 15–30 minutes. Repeat the process. Don't just be busy, be productive.

For the love of your work, take a break!

🛒 Checkout Counter

1. Think about three things you have been postponing for long. Does it fall under the big and scary bucket or the small and boring? List them here along with the category they belong to.

   a.

   b.

   c.

2. List all your activities on your to-do list into the Urgent/Important matrix:

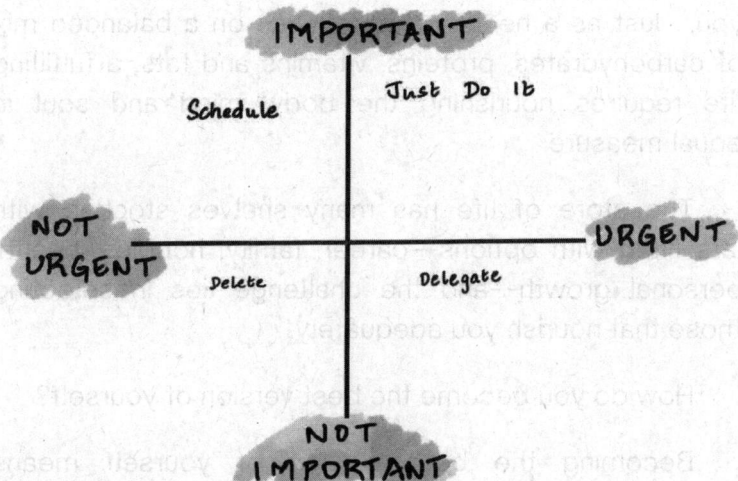

9
Maintain a Balanced Diet for the Body, Mind and Soul

Happy with that one giant packet of career in your basket? Or the massive box full of family?

No? You are not the only one. While a skewed basket may work for some, it is often balance that leads to a more content and fulfilling life. It isn't just about mindlessly adding items to your basket, but about thoughtfully choosing what nurtures and elevates you. Just as a healthy body thrives on a balanced mix of carbohydrates, proteins, vitamins and fats, a fulfilling life requires nourishing the body, mind and soul in equal measure.

The store of life has many shelves stocked with jars filled with options—career, family, hobbies, health, personal growth—and the challenge lies in selecting those that nourish you adequately.

How do you become the best version of yourself?

Becoming the best version of yourself means consciously feeding each area of your life with the right nourishment, every day. If you overstuff your basket with one thing, you risk neglecting the others, ultimately leading to imbalance. But when you make space for all the elements that contribute to your well-being, you begin to become a fuller, more grounded version of yourself.

How do you ensure that you are picking the right nourishment from the shelves?

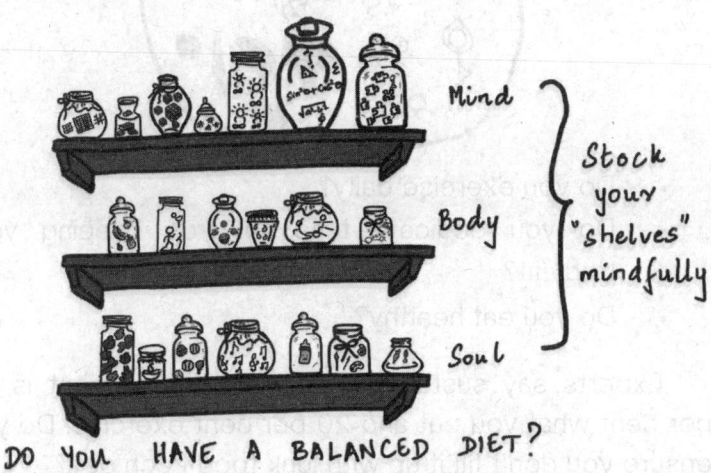

DO YOU HAVE A BALANCED DIET?

It starts with awareness—knowing which areas of your life need more focus, which need rest and which are already overflowing with goodness. Balance is not a one-time task; it is an ongoing process of consciously choosing what helps you grow, and ultimately help you become the best version of yourself.

In addition to the genes you inherit from your parents, having a healthy body is a function of how you take care of it.

Is your "Body Jar" as healthy as it can be?

- Do you exercise daily?
- Do you dedicate time towards keeping your body fit?
- Do you eat healthy?

Experts say sustainable weight management is 80 per cent what you eat and 20 per cent exercise. Do you ensure you don't fill it up with junk food each day?

Why? You may ask. Well, a healthy diet provides you with the necessary fuel to maintain a healthy life. As Jim Rohn rightly puts it, "Take care of your body, it is the only place you have to live."

In addition to exercise and healthy food, what else do you fill in your body jar? Ensure you get sufficient sleep. And bear a lightness of heart that allows you to laugh when you hear something funny or flash a smile when you spot something beautiful.

Typically, what goes in comes out, so do take a look at what you are feeding your body day in and day out.

What are you filling your "Mind Jar" with?

- Do you spend time each day towards sharpening your mind and keeping it at the top of its game?
- Do you participate in activities that improve your problem-solving skills or memory?
- When was the last time you read a book or solved a puzzle?
- When was the last time you learnt anything new?
- Does every day of your life look the same in terms of the activities you do?

If you found yourself hesitating or answering "no" to some of these questions, perhaps your mind jar could use a little sprucing up!

The other day I read something that provided an interesting perspective on this—"Curiosity will conquer fear even more than bravery will".

What's in your "Soul Jar"?

There is undeniable value in engaging in activities that bring you contentment. Seek out what truly makes you happy—things you do not do for approval, ego or fortune, but simply for the joy they bring you. Do them because in those moments, you feel connected to something greater than yourself. This is the essence of flow whether or not you believe in the concept.

- What makes you smile?
- What sets your soul on fire?
- What makes your spirit come alive?
- What soothes you in ways nothing else can?

Flow is that magical state when you are so immersed in an activity that time seems to disappear. It is the sweet spot where effort feels effortless, and everything around you falls into place.

- Does music transport you to a different place?
- Does coding and geeking out over a new software give you a kick like no other?
- Does writing make you happy?
- Is spending time in your garden, taking care of your plants the happiest time of the day for you?
- Is watching your child grow and helping her or him to evolve provide you the most satisfying moments of your life?

I am reminded of a dialogue the super-talented jazz musician Joe observed in the lovely movie *Soul*: "See, the tune is just an excuse to bring out the you."

Look within and fill your soul jar with things that make your soul smile.

As someone wise once said, "The mind is its thoughts, the heart is its desires and the soul is its experiences."

In the same way that a balanced diet requires a mix of nutrients for your body, your life needs a balance of nourishment for your body, mind and soul. Are you picking from each of life's shelves and stocking up each of your jars—physical health, mental enrichment and emotional or spiritual well-being? Just as an imbalanced meal can leave you feeling unsatisfied, an unbalanced life can lead to burnout. Ensure your cart is filled with what truly nourishes you, creating a harmonious blend that brings peace, contentment and meaning to your life.

Do you have a balanced life basket?

🛒 Checkout Counter

1. List things you do that enrich your body.

    a.

    b

    c.

2. List things you do that enrich your mind.

    a.

    b

    c.

3. List things you do that enrich your soul.

    a.

    b

    c.

10

Eat Mindfully

"Mindful eating is very pleasant. We sit beautifully. We are aware of the people surrounding us. We are aware of the food on our plates. This is a deep practice."
—Thich Nhat Hanh

Should you diet? Or fast intermittently? Or avoid meat? Or simply eat healthily?

What is the best diet for weight loss?

Yes, it is a trick question; the answer is none of them.

No matter your approach to food—it is essential to change how you relate to it.

Do you indulge in emotional eating as a way to cope with stress, boredom or sadness?

This often leads to guilt-ridden consumption.

On the other hand, conscious eating is about being fully present and intentional with each meal. Instead of obsessing over calories or constantly worrying about unhealthy choices, focus on the nourishment the food provides and the joy of eating. Pay attention to how your body feels, savour each bite and embrace the experience without distraction.

There are many benefits of conscious eating.

It not only improves your relationship with food but also enhances your mental well-being. As you shift from reacting to food out of habit or emotion, you start enjoying the act of eating and making empowered, balanced choices.

Realising how fortunate you are to have food on your plate and in practising gratitude for it naturally enhances the experience of eating. When you appreciate every meal that you partake, it nourishes your body and uplifts your spirit.

Eat to fuel your body, not feed your emotions.

As you savour each morsel mindfully, notice how it feels on your tongue, enjoy the texture with full attention and taste every flavour. Immerse yourself in the moment and let the act of eating become a joyful experience. Mindful eating transforms a routine meal into a moment of connection with yourself.

Disconnect from devices when you eat, so that you can completely focus on eating and staying in the present moment. Eating without distractions not only enhances your enjoyment but also fosters a deeper connection with your body's cues and your food.

Try a simple trick at home: Appreciate one thing about the meal you are having each time you sit at the table. If someone else has made the meal, voice your appreciation. See how their expression changes and see how your mood changes as well. I bet the food will get digested so much better too!

Make mealtimes an opportunity not just to nourish your body, but also to connect with those around you. In today's fast-paced world, it is easy to eat while distracted—scrolling through your phone, watching TV or rushing through a meal to move on to the next task. Instead, create a space where you give your food and the people at your table the attention they deserve. When you eat mindfully, you become more present, allowing you to truly engage with your companions. Use this time to share stories, listen and build connections.

We have a "rule" in our house: no phones and no books at the dining table. The number of stories I have heard my daughter recount at the table is perhaps only second to the number of stories she tells me when it is time for her to go to bed, and she has to tell me more stories so that she can delay her bedtime! I know which child gets into trouble with the principal regularly; I know which one loves maths; and I know which one recently got a secret tattoo her parents know nothing about!

Similarly, with my husband I know of the enthusiastic fresher who mails my husband on the weekend asking for work because he doesn't have enough; I know the colleague who makes the best biryani; and I know the co-worker who is eager to start his own business.

They too have become part of my family because of our dinner-table conversations, and I am able to connect with the people that matter to my family in a more meaningful way.

The simple act of eating together can become a meaningful experience, where the focus shifts from simply filling your stomach to savouring both the food and the relationships. Sharing meals mindfully not only enhances the joy of eating, but also strengthens bonds, turning an ordinary activity into a cherished experience that nourishes both your body and the soul.

Checkout Counter

1. Which meal of the day will you choose to keep your gadgets away?

2. Try mindfully eating your meals for the next three days and note down any changes you may have experienced within yourself.

    a.

    b.

    c.

    d.

11
Create s p a c e

Cane may give a basket its shape, clay may shape the pot, but it is the emptiness inside that holds whatever we want. You may be tempted to fill your basket of life to the brim but it is equally important to create the space to "be".

It's cane that shapes the basket...

...but it's the emptiness inside that holds whatever we want

While in the above examples, space is a physical element, you may want to think about the various ways space plays itself out in other aspects.

Does your brain have too many tabs open?

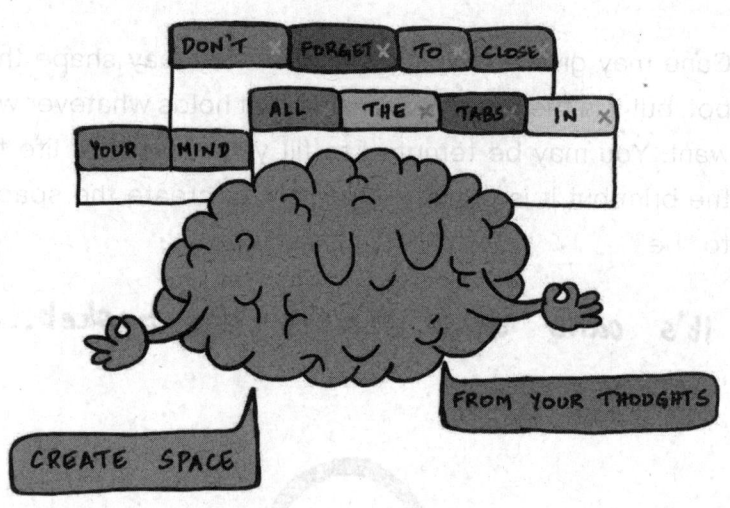

For instance, create space in your mind from the constant ebb and flow of thoughts so that you can bring your focus on the present moment. You could do that by watching your breath, observing nature, meditation, exercise, sport, or by any other means that works for you. Creating space in the mind is important to let new ideas flow in, to tap into your creative reserves and to give yourself some extra room to think.

Create space to bloom

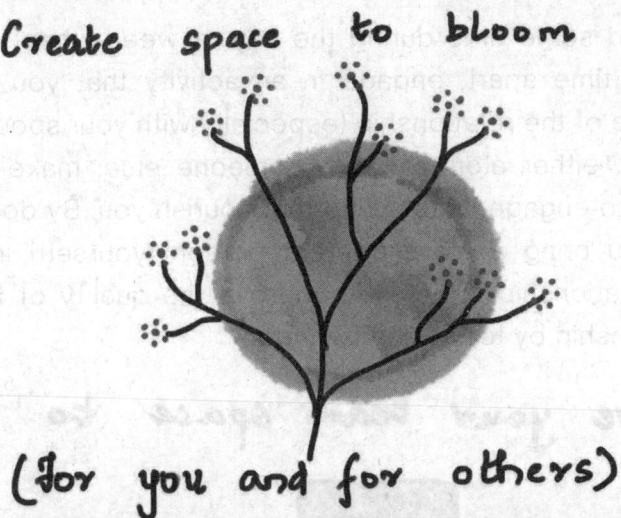

(for you and for others)

Giving people space in any relationship, be it with your spouse, parents, kids or friends can do things that nourish their souls. A content person brings contentment to a relationship. And contentment is often found in solitude.

"The soul needs more space than the body."—Axel Munthe

Maintain healthy space in all

your relationships, especially personal

Find some time during the day or week when you spend time apart; engage in an activity that you do outside of the relationship (especially with your spouse or kid), either alone or with someone else; make an effort to engage in activities that nourish you. By doing so, you bring a more content person (yourself) into the relationship, which will improve the quality of the relationship by leaps and bounds.

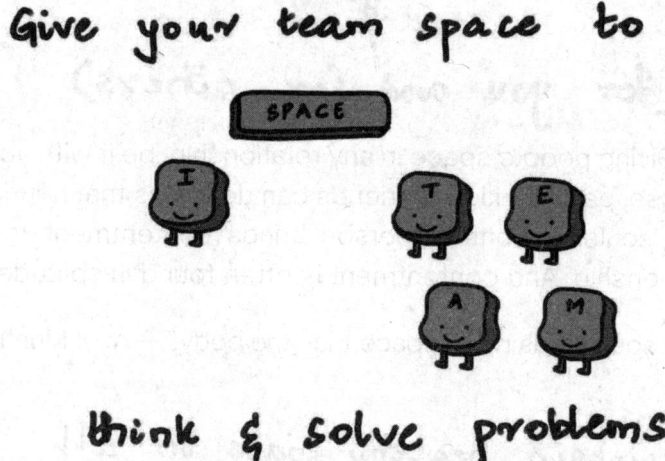

Creating space is equally crucial in your workspace, especially when it comes to fostering growth and independence within a team. Micromanaging or constantly supervising every task can stifle creativity and undermine confidence. Instead, offering your team members the autonomy to think critically and solve problems on their own demonstrates trust and empowers them to take ownership of their work.

One practical example could be delegating the creation of a project timeline to a junior team member. While you remain available for guidance, letting them take the lead allows them to build confidence in their planning and coordination abilities. When the team sees their efforts bearing fruit—whether it is a successful launch or a well-executed initiative—it reinforces their sense of competence and motivates them to take on greater challenges in the future.

By creating this space, you cultivate a team that is not only more productive but also more self-reliant and engaged, ultimately leading to better overall outcomes for everyone involved.

Is creating space about stepping back?

No, it is about fostering an environment where both you and those around you can thrive and grow. For yourself, it might mean carving out time for reflection, creativity or simply rest—moments that nurture your soul and allow you to align with your true aspirations. For others, it means offering trust, encouragement and the freedom to explore their potential without fear of failure.

When you create this space, you enable transformation—both your own and that of those around you. It is in this openness that people, ideas and possibilities bloom. Ultimately, creating space is about becoming—becoming more aligned with your purpose, more connected to others, and more in tune with the beautiful process of growth and change.

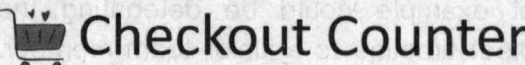 Checkout Counter

1. Think about the important relationships in your life. Do you feel you give the other person enough space? Is the relationship as wholesome and positive as it could be?

2. If the answer is no, think about three ways in which you could give yourself and the other person some space.

12

Declutter Your Life

Tired of looking at a dirty house?

Simple.

Just turn off the lights.

On a serious note, having fewer possessions gives you more freedom and flexibility with your options. An uncluttered life promotes mental clarity and peace. A clear mind is a great way to fill your basket of life with things that truly bring you contentment.

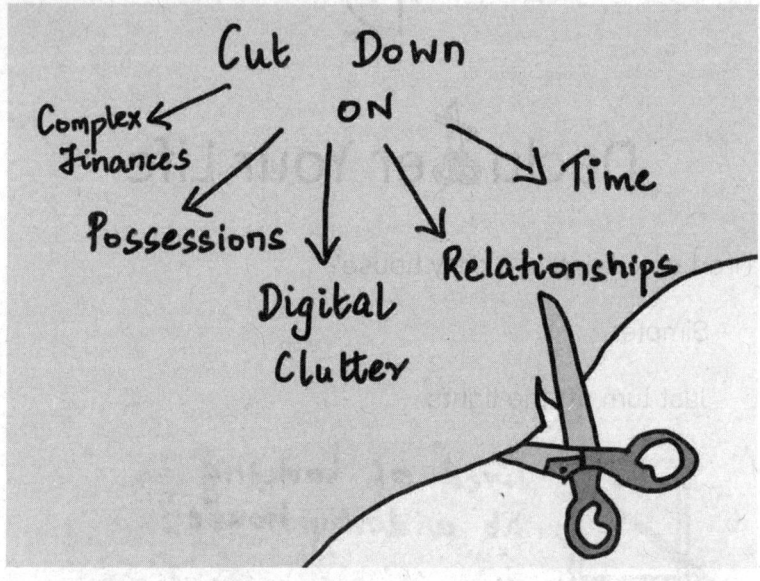

People tend to immediately think of material possessions when they hear the word "declutter", but minimalism can be practised in many areas especially in the following five:

- physical clutter,
- digital clutter,
- relationship clutter,
- financial clutter, and
- time clutter.

After all, the less you have the less you have to clean.

"Hangxiety" is simply not worth it. What's that? The stress that comes from hanging onto stuff you don't need.

If you don't love or use it, that is clutter.

Declutter physically

Have you ever noticed how getting rid of things automatically makes you feel lighter?

The fewer possessions you own, the lighter you feel. And there is nothing unbearable about this lightness, my friend.

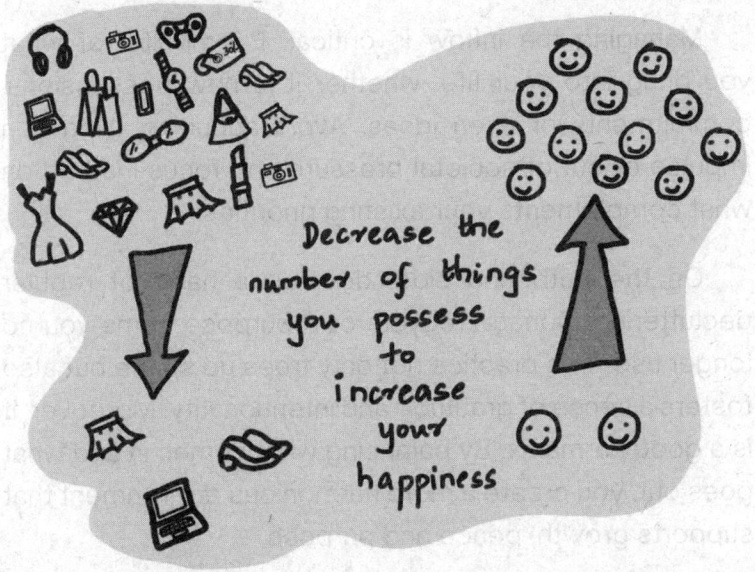

Are you one of those who pursues one pleasure after another without experiencing any material change in happiness?

Stop!

Think.

Pare down to the essentials and manage both the inflow and outflow of possessions to maintain balance and clarity in your life. Start by assessing what truly adds value to your daily living—items that serve a purpose or bring you joy. Let go of things that no longer align with your needs or goals, creating physical and mental space for what truly matters.

Managing the inflow is critical. Be mindful of what you bring into your life, whether it is new possessions, commitments or even ideas. Avoid acquiring things on impulse or out of societal pressure and focus instead on what complements your existing priorities.

On the outbound side, develop a habit of regular decluttering. Donate, recycle or repurpose items you no longer use. This practice not only frees up space but also fosters a sense of gratitude and intentionality. Moreover, it is a good karma fix. By balancing what comes in and what goes out, you create a more harmonious environment that supports growth, peace and purpose.

Be mindful of what goes into your basket. Here is the checklist:

1. Choose quality over quantity.
2. Have fewer items but give them more love.
3. Cherish the few things you do possess.

Love decorating your house with a dozen cheap trinkets? How about investing in a single handcrafted piece of art that resonates with your personality or has a meaningful story behind it?

This approach not only reduces clutter but also deepens your connection with the items you own. Each time you look at that cherished piece, it brings joy and a sense of purpose, far outweighing the fleeting satisfaction of accumulating many forgettable objects.

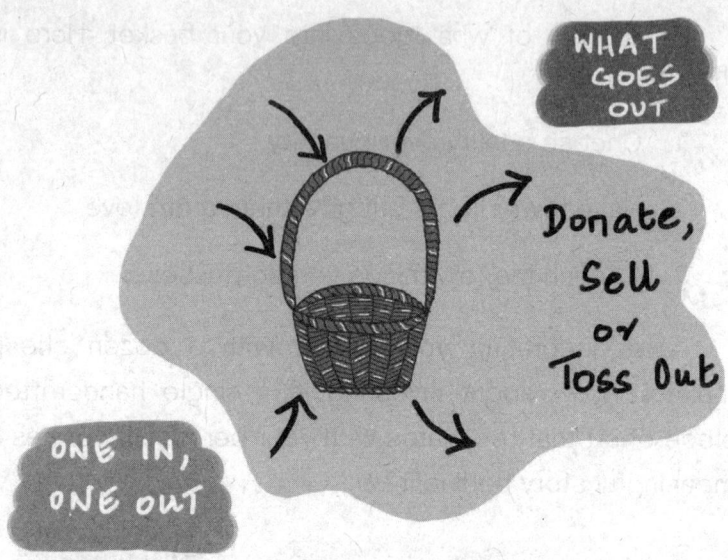

With outbound items, I try following one rule—when I buy one item, I try to donate, sell or toss another out of my basket of life. That way, I am left with the same number of items in my basket.

Try it.

Declutter digitally

"I find myself seeing the world through a screen and not my eyes."—Ed Sheeran

Does this resonate with you?

With every passing year, do you seem to be spending more and more time in the digital world than you ever have in the past?

Disconnect to connect.

Because minimising digital clutter promotes mental well-being. Your digital environment either produces clarity or adds to the complexity and anguish of your mental state.

A study at the University of Pennsylvania found that high usage of Facebook, Snapchat and Instagram increases feelings of loneliness. The 2018 study found that reducing social media use to 30 minutes a day resulted in a significant reduction in levels of anxiety, depression, loneliness, sleep problems and FOMO (fear of missing out).

No posting.

No liking.

Just living.

Losing sleep already?

Relax. You don't need to cut back on your social media use that drastically to improve your mental health. The same study concluded that just being more mindful of your social media use can have beneficial results on your mood and focus.

I am sure you will agree. Constantly pinging notifications from the dozens of apps on your digital devices distracts from any productive work that you are trying to do and

Reduce your digital clutter

takes away your focus from what is crucial like having a real conversation with your loved one. When was the last time you had one?

Technology should improve your life, not become your life.

How do you go about it, though?

Turning off notifications is the easiest way to minimise digital clutter so that you can choose when you want to check on your apps rather than the apps being the master of your time.

Put that phone down and pick up your life!

Other simple tasks you can try are using a password manager to take away the burden of remembering and managing passwords with their complex rules, instead of keeping it all in your head, or worse still, saved on an Excel sheet or Notepad.

You can also tidy up your images by offloading them to the cloud so that your device is light and clean. For instance, set up email rules to automatically sort promotional emails into a separate folder, ensuring that your primary inbox is reserved for important messages. This keeps your inbox organised and reduces the stress of sifting through clutter to find what truly matters.

Use a password manager

Tidy your phone by offloading to cloud

Declutter your relationships

"Old ways won't open new doors."

I don't know who said that, but it is important to evaluate your relationships from time to time.

Does that friend or relative of yours energise you or drain you?

If it is the latter, the solution is simple.

Choose wisely about who you give the precious gift of your time to.

Spend more time with people who energise you

And less time with those who drain you of your energy

Why spend time with those who drain your energy and steal the joy out of living? If that friend of yours constantly complains, criticises, or makes you feel undervalued, consider reducing the time you spend with them.

Be done with people. Not mad. Not bothered. Just done.

Instead, invest that energy in relationships that uplift you, such as a friend who encourages your growth or a family member who always brings positivity to your conversations. Create more space for meaningful connections that nourish your well-being.

And if you're energised by some alone time, block time to be by yourself

Or if you are the sort of person who derives energy from being alone, make sure you slot time for yourself.

Declutter your financial space

Simplify your finances.

I cannot state it more simply.

Time is the one finite resource you have, and if you want to maximise your contentment in the limited time you are given, it is worth using your money to buy back some of that precious time. Whether it is outsourcing tasks like house cleaning or grocery shopping or investing in appliances like a dishwasher or a robotic vacuum cleaner, these small financial investments can save you hours.

Use your money to buy time

You could spend that extra time on something more meaningful, like pursuing a hobby, connecting with loved ones or simply relaxing.

Unless you are the sort who thinks *What is the use of happiness if it can't buy you money?*

Money certainly can't buy more time, but you can certainly spend your money in a way that allows you to enjoy more of it!

How about unsubscribing from something you have not used for more than three months? Unused subscriptions drain your pocket while adding nothing meaningful to your life.

Cancel unused subscriptions

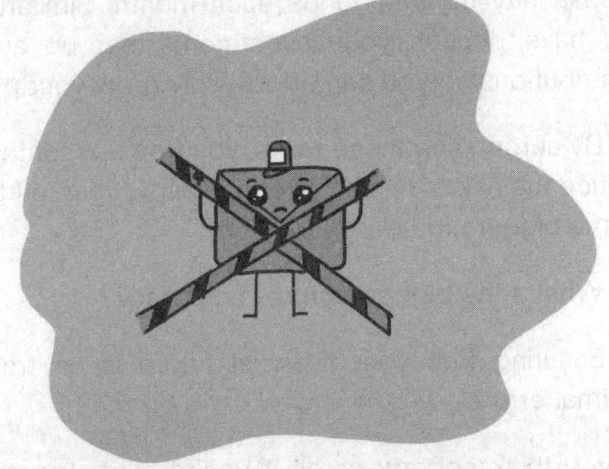

Automate your bills, savings and investments once you have done the smart work of pruning your list and knowing exactly what you want to invest in and spend money on. Automate your savings to ensure that you are

Automate your bills, investments & savings

consistently building your future wealth, without having to manually transfer funds each month. Similarly, once you have chosen your investments, set up automatic contributions so you can effortlessly grow your portfolio.

By automating these tasks, you free up mental space, reduce the risk of human error and allow yourself to focus on the bigger picture.

What's the bigger picture? Lost track?

Ensuring that your financial future is on track with minimal effort.

"If you think nobody cares if you're alive, try missing a couple of car payments."—Earl Wilson

Are you one of those who constantly keeps having an out-of-money experience?

Is it because you have many debts to pay off?

Try the Avalanche method. No, this avalanche will not result in disastrous consequences.

Here is how it goes:

Pay off the debt with the highest interest rate first, then the one with the second highest interest rate and so on. This works on the premise that you have the money to pay off (even slightly) more than the minimum payment needed for each of the debts. Increase your extra payments as you pay off your debts.

The Avalanche method works because it targets the most expensive debt first—debt with the highest interest rate—allowing you to save money on interest over time. When you pay off the debt with the highest interest rate first, you reduce the amount of interest you are being charged, which in turn accelerates your ability to pay down other debts more quickly. By focusing on this high-interest debt and making larger payments than the minimum, you are actively reducing the balance more effectively and stopping it from accumulating interest at a faster rate. Once the highest-interest debt is paid off, you move to the next highest, and so on, which builds momentum. This approach can help you pay off your total debt faster and save more money in the long run.

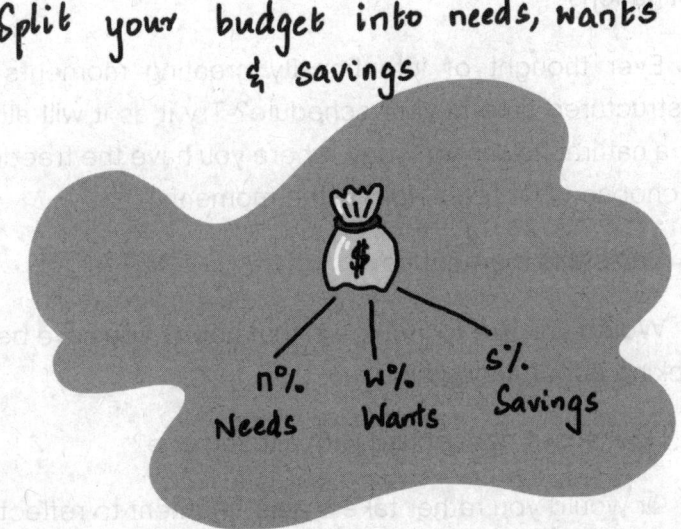

Manage your finances based on your wants, needs and savings. While you can split your finances in any portions across those buckets, it is good to save for each of these. Finance experts usually suggest a 50:30:20 split across these categories.

Declutter your time

Decluttering allows you to step away from the overwhelming busyness of life and avoid feeling like you are just going through the motions. It gives you the opportunity to engage with life in a more present, intentional way.

Is your schedule filled with back-to-back tasks or obligations?

Ever thought of intentionally creating moments of unstructured time in your schedule? Try it as it will allow for a natural flow in your day, where you have the freedom to choose what feels *right* in the moment.

Seize this moment now.

Would you like to indulge in that hobby you have been thinking about a long time?

How about connecting with a loved one?

Or would you rather take a quiet moment to reflect?

Having that space creates a rhythm in your life that supports well-being and joy. By clearing away the noise and the constant rush, you can focus on what truly matters—nourishing your relationships, investing in self-care or pursuing passions that bring you fulfilment.

Create open, unstructured space in your life

In our fast-paced, productivity-driven world, we are often so focused on "doing"—checking off tasks, meeting deadlines and staying busy—that we forget the importance of "being" and "non-doing".

I cannot stress this enough—these moments of non-doing are essential to your mental and physical well-being.

It is not wasteful to carve out time for nothing in particular.

Pause. Reset and process the constant flow of information and activity around us. Either you run the day or the day runs you.

Block time for non-doing

When we allow ourselves time to simply "be", without the pressure to accomplish anything, we give our nervous systems the chance to relax. This practice helps to reduce stress, recharge our energy and improve our overall mental clarity. As the Dalai Lama once wisely said, "We are human beings not human doings."

I am not advocating idleness or disengagement, but stepping away from the hustle, allowing your thoughts to settle and reconnecting with the present moment. Don't succumb to the toxic effects of grind and hustle culture.

When you create space for creativity, reflection and inner peace, you enhance your ability to tackle the tasks that really matter with focus and intentionality. By integrating non-doing into your life, you can restore balance and cultivate a steadier, more grounded sense of self.

What new can I say about social media addiction and its pitfalls that you don't know already?

Less scrolling and more living prevent burnout and mental fatigue. It also allows you to reclaim your time, focus on the present and nurture real-life relationships. Stop sharing memes and ignoring people, especially the ones who matter.

The chapter on disconnecting delves deeper into this, offering practical habits and strategies to help create boundaries with digital distractions and find balance in a hyper-connected world. The quickest way to restore your mental peace and build a healthier, more mindful relationship with technology is to simply step away. No, you don't have to post it to prove it. Offline is peace of mind.

What does your typical workday look like?

Do you spend a lot of time in meetings?

What percentage of that could have been handled just as effectively through an email or a text?

Can you accept fewer meetings and set up fewer meetings to utilise your time in a more fruitful manner?

Accept fewer meetings

Learning to say "no" to non-priorities frees up time and energy to say "yes" to the right things. We have already discussed this in the chapter on the power of saying "no". Mastering the art of saying "no" is crucial for managing your time, energy and mental health.

As you practise this skill, you will find yourself more focused, with a clearer sense of purpose and the freedom to prioritize what truly deserves your attention.

And now, a little personal story.

Having a child was like being handed a brutally honest performance review—except this one came with sticky fingers and an uncanny ability to repeat my worst habits. Kids don't do what you say, they do what you do. That terrifying truth hit me like a rogue LEGO underfoot, and suddenly, decluttering wasn't just about tidying up—it was about making room for the things that actually mattered.

With time more precious than my last piece of chocolate, I had to be ruthless. I ditched the fast lane of strategy consulting for a more grounded analytics role. Notifications? Off. TV? Non-existent for 16 years. Phone? Silenced for 90 minutes after work, because nothing says "I love you" like actually listening. Like all working mums, I worried about not spending enough time with my child. But I figured fewer hours, filled with undistracted presence, love and life, were far better than a whole day of half-hearted attention.

And so, I decluttered—not just my space, but my time, my mind and my priorities. It wasn't always easy, but it was worth it.

Which brings me back to the heart of this chapter. Here's the mantra:

~~Should.~~

~~Would.~~

~~Could.~~

DID.

🛒 Checkout Counter

1. List one thing you will do under each area which will help declutter your life:

    a. Physical Clutter:

    b. Digital Clutter:

    c. Financial Clutter:

    d. Relationship Clutter:

    e. Time Clutter:

13

Find What You Are Looking For

If I asked you to count the number of red cars you spot on the road today before you leave your house, you will end up noticing red cars more than you usually do. Similarly, if you were asked to count the number of white flowers you spot around you all day, you will notice them a lot more than you usually would have.

If I asked you to count the number of red cars you see on the road today...

...or the number of white flowers you see...

You will end up noticing red cars or white flowers because that is where your focus is.

Why do you think that is?

Someone asked you to be aware of them and you brought that to the top of your mind.

You will observe you notice red cars and white flowers more than you usually do because that's where your focus is

What are you training your mind to notice?

Have you observed that the world often seems full of a certain kind of people or experiences?

What are you training your mind to notice?

Acts of kindness?

Or everything that is wrong around you?

Could it be because you have subconsciously trained your mind to focus only on those patterns?

Our minds function as powerful filters, constantly processing and interpreting the vast amount of information we encounter daily. Whether we're aware of it or not, we tend to focus on the things that align with our thoughts, beliefs and expectations. This is why, if you're focused on negativity, for example, you'll often find more negative experiences, or if you are set on achieving a particular goal, you notice opportunities that might have otherwise passed you by.

Shifting your focus can dramatically alter the way you perceive the world around you. When you choose to look for positivity, solutions or new opportunities, your mind starts to highlight those, making them more apparent and accessible. In this way, you can open yourself up to new possibilities and perspectives, embracing a more expansive and enriching view of life. The act of consciously directing your attention can help you step beyond your habitual thought patterns and into a space of greater awareness and possibility.

You usually find what you're looking for!

🛒 Checkout Counter

Introspect about what you usually see in the world around you. Do you think you have opened yourself up to newer possibilities? Observe yourself when you are placed in such a situation today and find out what else you see.

14

Get Better with ~~Prastice~~ ~~Practise~~ Practice

It is a well-established fact that you get better with whatever you practice. People from various fields have spoken about the rigorous hours of practice they put in every single day in their chosen field over the years of their life to get to the pinnacle of their career.

While this fact has been explored in sports, arts, science and others, have you thought about how it is equally applicable to your thought patterns and mental well-being?

If your mind were a lab, and your thoughts the inputs into the process that determined the quality of your life, it seems logical that what goes in repeatedly has the maximum impact on the output.

Unstable compound: complaining carbonate (CoCO3)

The more you complain, the better you get at it. Even when you are presented with a neutral scenario, you will find a reason to complain because you have had so much practice complaining.

Think of it like shopping—if you always reach for the same items on the shelf, over time, it becomes second nature. Without realising it, you may find yourself

picking up complaints as if they were essentials on your shopping list, stocking your basket with negativity instead of solutions.

While it is incredibly easy to blame the external situation and think the fault lies entirely in what is happening on the outside, it is crucial to take the focus inwards and check if you are so used to reacting in one particular manner that you are unable to view the situation through any lens other than the one you have practised a million times in the past.

Have you practised complaining so much that you have become a complaining carbonate? How does that make you feel on the inside? Maybe it is time to rethink what you are adding to your basket.

Stable compound: positive phosphate (PoPO4)

Most situations have a mix of positives and negatives—just like a shopping trip where some items are great finds while others might not be exactly what you wanted. If you start training your mind to focus on the best picks in any situation, over time, you will naturally become someone who can spot the good, no matter what life puts on the shelves in front of you.

Stable Compound: Positive Phosphate ($PoPO_4$)

Life Flask

Think about the people in your life—some exude warmth, effortlessly lifting the mood of those around them. If you observe them closely, you will notice that they have mastered the habit of selecting optimism, much like a seasoned shopper who knows how to fill their cart with value rather than clutter. They have practised this mindset for so long that it has become second nature. In other words, they are the positive phosphates of your world, enriching every interaction.

So, how do you train your mind to be more optimistic? After all, a well-stocked mind—just like a well-stocked basket—makes life easier. And really, what's the point of taking life so seriously? You'll never get out of it alive!

Simple compound: selfless sulphate (SeSO4)

If you are presented with a choice and you choose to be selfless once, it is like picking a high-quality item off the shelf—one that adds lasting value. The next time, it gets easier to make the same choice because of the positive feedback loop you receive, much like returning to a trusted brand that never disappoints. Over time, selflessness becomes second nature, a go-to selection in the way you navigate life.

Be a happy memory for everyone. As you practise selflessness more often, it becomes a staple in your basket, a choice you make effortlessly.

When you pour selflessness into the flask of life, it fills up with the simple yet invaluable compound—selfless sulphate.

Pure compound: honest hydroxide Ho(OH)2

"No legacy is so rich as honesty."—William Shakespeare

As with all the other traits you can add to the flask of life, honesty is like a premium ingredient that you can choose to stock up or take the easier route with cheaper substitutes. The first time you are faced with a situation where dishonesty seems like the simpler option, it might feel uncomfortable to choose the truth. But much like investing in a high-quality product instead of a fleeting

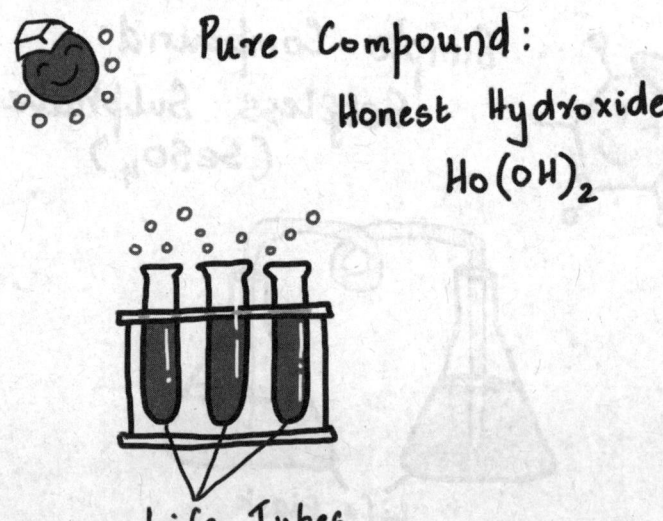

bargain, making the harder choice now leads to greater rewards in the long run.

And the more you practise being genuine, the more natural that choice becomes—just like consistently choosing wholesome, high-quality ingredients over artificial fillers. Before you know it, your life's shopping cart is stocked with the purest essentials, and your life lab is filled with the simple yet powerful compound of honest hydroxide.

What do you practise regularly? What habits, thoughts or behaviours are you unknowingly perfecting day after day? The things we repeatedly do, think and feel quietly shape us, often without our awareness. If you constantly dwell on worries, you might unintentionally become skilled at finding problems where there may be none. If you practise kindness, even in small ways, you will naturally foster warmth and compassion in your interactions.

Take a moment to ask yourself:

Are my daily practices aligning with the person I want to become?

Are my habits and behaviours serving me well, or are they pulling me away from the version of myself I aspire to be?

Maybe it is time to get to the checkout counter of your life, lay out everything you have been adding to your basket, and reflect.

Are you stocking up on what truly nourishes you, or have you been picking up things out of habit that no longer serve you?

It is never too late to change what you practise! Once you are aware of what fills your time and thoughts, you can choose to invest in actions and attitudes that bring meaning, joy and growth.

After all, life is shaped by what we practise, and the practice we choose today shapes the person we become tomorrow.

🛒 Checkout Counter

1. Think about the five instances where you felt highs or lows in the past. What did you exhibit? Is that something you practise often? Is there something you would like to change or start inculcating within?

2. List two traits you want to start practising more consciously:

    a.

    b.

15

Disc⊘nnect to Stay Co∩∩ected

A recent study has shown millennials in the US spend more than five hours each day on their phone. Add eight hours of laptop usage and another two hours of television/screen time, that is a whopping 15 hours of screen time per day, or 98 per cent of the waking time. This study revealed that the Baby Boomers aren't far behind, and here in India, we are not too different either. The numbers paint a vivid picture of just how tethered we have become to our screens.

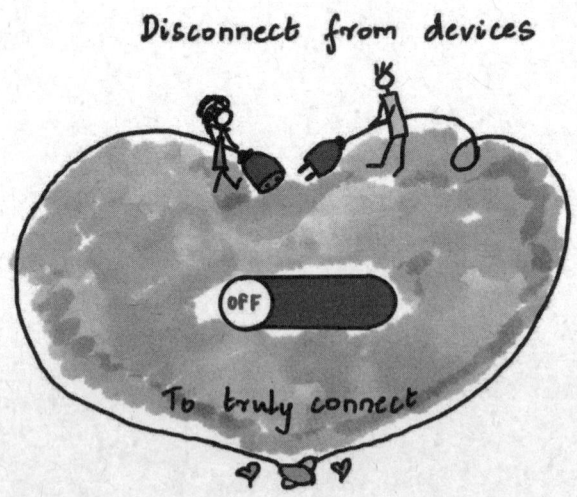

You are constantly connected to your devices, but are you connected to yourself and to your loved ones?

What steps have you taken to consciously stay away from the habit?

Habits are like the items you keep adding to your shopping cart—some nourish you, while others just take up space. The key is to stock up on the ones that truly add value to your life.

Let's explore what habits we can build to step away from the endless aisles of social media and instead invest in meaningful connections—with ourselves and our loved ones.

Choose when you want to connect

Can you count the number of times every hour your thoughts have been interrupted by some notification on your phone? Have you thought about how long it takes to get back to your chain of thoughts and take them to a meaningful conclusion after having been distracted by the notification?

One effective habit to not be consumed by your mobile phone is turning notifications off. Why not choose to be the mistress of your destiny and decide when you want to check your phone? You can either set a pre-determined time to check on your social media apps or do it at a time of leisure so that it does not chew into your productive time, either at work or when with friends and family.

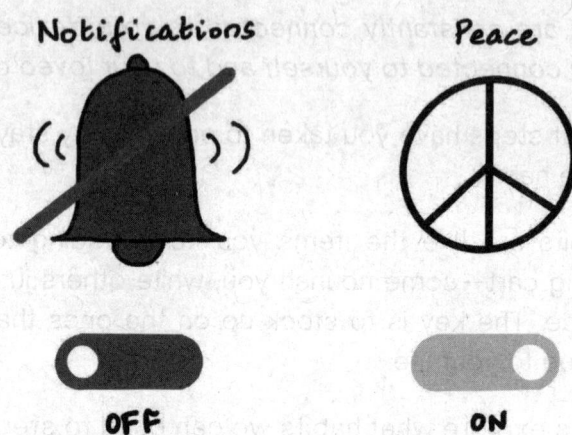

Digital wellness isn't about abstaining from technology; it is about using it in a way that supports your well-being and enhances your life. Once you practise digital mindfulness you consciously choose how you engage with technology rather than letting it dictate your life.

Have a gadget-free start to the day

Alpha brainwaves are typically present when you are in a state of relaxed alertness, meaning you are awake, but not performing mentally taxing tasks. Relaxed alertness is what you experience when you first wake up in the morning. Do you want to be spending that precious mental state on mind-numbing consumption of content spewed by your smartphone or use it for more meaningful pursuits such as creating something new, meditating/exercising or setting the tone for the rest of the day or connecting with your loved ones?

A small habit such as promising yourself not to use the phone for 30 minutes after you wake up can go a long way in energising yourself at the very start of the day that usually has a lasting effect on the rest of your day too.

Practise a gadget-free hour at home

Similarly, try staying away from gadgets for the first hour after you return home from work. Instead of scrolling through your phone or checking emails, use this time to reconnect with your loved ones or simply spend some quality moments with yourself. Talk to your family about their day, share your own experiences or enjoy a meal together without any digital distractions.

If you are alone, indulge in activities that rejuvenate you—read a book, meditate or step out for a walk.

This intentional break from technology not only fosters stronger relationships, but also helps you decompress and transition from work mode to home mode, bringing a sense of balance and harmony to your day. Head to the Mind, Body and Soul shelves, and fill each jar with items to make them stronger.

Reduce the time watching television

"Television is a weapon of mass distraction."—Larry Gelbart

Ever thought about getting rid of the television altogether? As a family, we went without a television for 16 years, and that decision created time and space to explore new interests and develop fulfilling habits. During this period, we learnt to play chess, mastered solving the Rubik's cube, our daughter picked up canvas painting, we learnt two new languages and each of us finished at least three books a month.

Sounds too drastic?

Disconnecting from digital devices is not about abandoning the modern world but about reclaiming the precious time and energy they so effortlessly consume. You only have so much room in your basket of life. If you fill it entirely with digital distractions, there will be no space left for the rich experiences of life. By stepping away from screens, you make room to shop for more meaningful interactions, hobbies that bring joy and moments of quiet reflection.

"Remote controls are quite handy. They let you see that there's nothing worth watching on TV a lot faster."—Melanie White

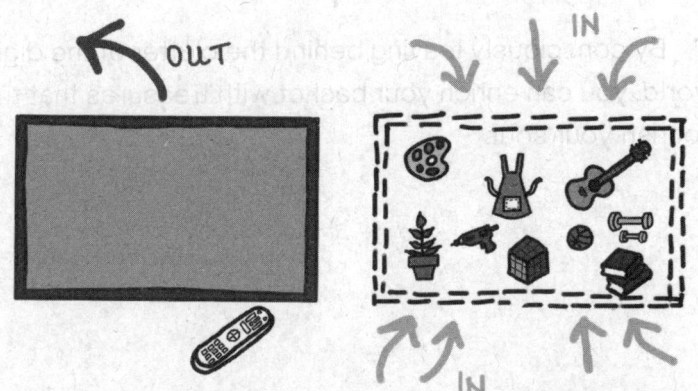

REDUCE TV VIEWING TIME... OUT IN IN ...AND SEE HOW MUCH SPACE GETS CREATED FOR NEW EXPERIENCES

The average television occupies about 750 square inches on the wall but takes up exponentially more space in your mind—about 20,000 square inches, figuratively speaking. Even if there is nothing specific you want to watch, its mere presence invites you to turn it on, and before you know it, an hour of your precious time has been spent consuming whatever it offers. Families with a second television in the bedroom often find themselves dealing with chaos, reduced connection and an overload of unnecessary information that clutters even the quietest corners of the mind.

Each notification you ignore is like choosing not to pick up the junk food on the shelf, and each hour spent device-free is an investment in the premium goods of life—quality time, deeper connections and inner peace.

What do you choose?

By consciously leaving behind the clutter of the digital world, you can enrich your basket with treasures that truly nourish your soul.

🛒 Checkout Counter

1. Keep a log of the days you went without your gadgets in the morning and in the evening. Check to see how you felt at the end of those days.

2. Compare it against the days when you checked the gadgets and jot down the noticeable difference (s) in yourself.

3. List three activities you will do instead of being on your gadgets once you get back home at the end of the day.

    a.

    b.

    c.

16
Stay in the Here and Now

"If you are at peace, you are living in the present."
—Lao Tzu

Have you ever examined your thoughts? What do you notice? Do they wander like a shopper aimlessly browsing through aisles, picking up random items without a list?

To stay focused and achieve your goals, it is important to be intentional—just as a mindful shopper sticks to what

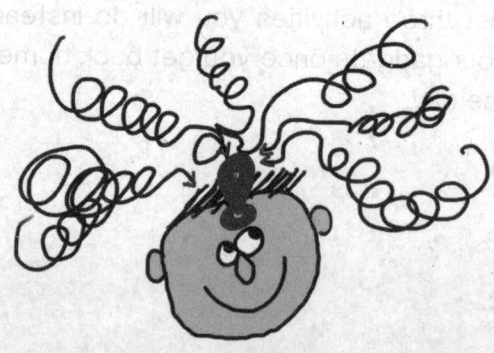

No matter where your mind wanders...

...You are always HERE

truly matters. No matter how far your mind drifts, your physical presence is always in the "here", right where you are at that moment.

Similarly, your thoughts may dwell in the past or in the future, but the only moment that is real and not in your head, is the present moment.

At any given moment, it is always NOW

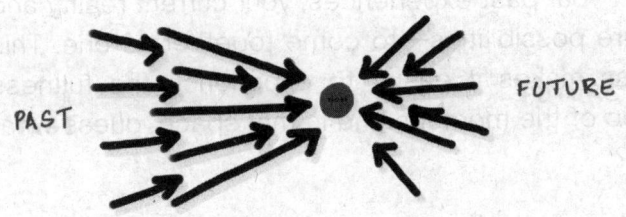

Everything else only exists in the mind

Catching your mind when it starts to wander and gently guiding it back to the present moment is a powerful practice. It is like reining in an unruly child with patience and care, helping him focus on the beauty and opportunities of the here and now.

As Eckhart Tolle beautifully puts it, "The key to transformation is to make friends with this moment. It doesn't matter what form it takes. Say yes to it. Allow it and be with it."

Make friends with this moment, irrespective of the form it takes

When you are fully present, you allow all parts of yourself—your past experiences, your current reality and your future possibilities—to come together as one. This wholeness makes it easier to experience the fullness and magic of the moment, and in that space, guess what happens?

True transformation.

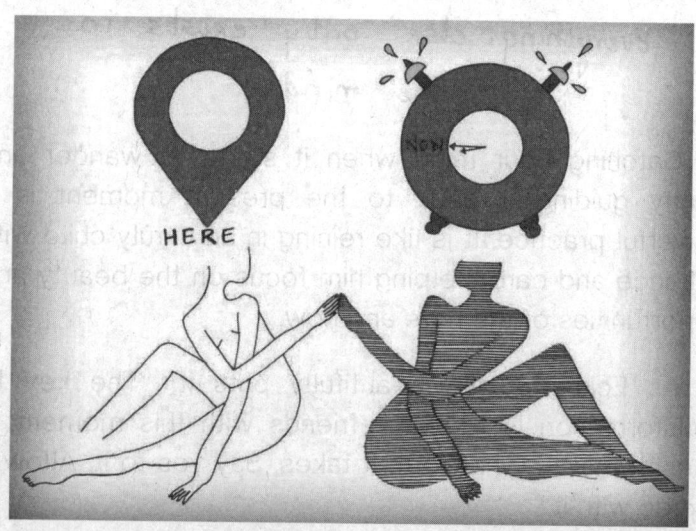

In embracing the present, you connect with the entirety of who you are and open yourself up to the deeper wisdom and peace that reside within you. Inhale the present moment, exhale the past.

So how do you go about bringing your attention to the present moment? Let us examine a few techniques to help you with this.

Watch your breath

"Feelings come and go like clouds in a windy sky. Conscious breathing is my anchor."—Thich Nhat Hanh

One of the most fundamental techniques used in meditation is watching your breath. No matter where your thoughts travel to, the breath is always grounded to the present moment.

When you focus on your breath, feel the coolness of the air when you inhale and feel the warmness as you exhale, for in that fraction of a moment, you are completely in the here and now.

As your mind wanders, bring your attention back to your breath without judging the thought. Acknowledge the thought as a friend, know that it too shall pass and bring your focus back to the breath.

One way to increase your concentration is to focus on the narrow region below your nostrils as you breathe. This small area of focus sharpens your attention and the ability to stay in the moment.

Exercise and feel your body

"When you do walking meditation, you are not just walking. You are walking and you are alive. You are aware of your breathing, aware of your body, aware of your surroundings. Walking is an exercise, but also a meditation."

—Thich Nhat Hanh

Think of a time when you held a yogasana for a minute or did 50 reps of an intense exercise or lifted some heavy weights at the gym. Do you ever worry about something other than completing the exercise or giving your body some respite from the pain?

Feel your body as you exercise to stay in the HERE and NOW

It is almost impossible for the mind to wander when it is made acutely aware of an intense sensation in the body. For those few minutes, the mind and body are completely in the present.

Play a sport to focus on the present

"I play the game the way I live my life—I live in the moment. When I'm on the court, I'm fully focused and everything else disappears. It's like meditation—you're just in the flow."
—Michael Jordan

When you play a game, where is your entire focus?

It is drawn to the immediate moment—you must react to what is happening in real time, whether it is a ball coming towards you, a player to outmanoeuvre or a strategy to execute.

Play a sport to focus on the HERE and NOW

Engaging in a physical sport is one of the most effective ways to anchor your mind in the present. A physical game instantly immerses you in the present, leaving no room for distractions. The rhythm of the game forces your mind to be fully present, creating a natural form of meditation through movement. The act of playing itself brings you into focus, where the mind and body work as one in the now. Concentration can be a fine antidote to anxiety.

If you feel muscle memory kicking in and don't feel the need to focus to react to the game, maybe it is time to pick up a new one or change the rules to add an element of newness to it. The idea is to engage in a physical activity that also activates the mind and not let it get into an autopilot mode.

Practise fasting to zoom to the present

"Fasting is not just about abstaining from food, it is a way to sharpen the mind and make the body more receptive. It creates a certain stillness within, which is what meditation is all about."—Sadhguru

While the health benefits of fasting are well-chronicled, its contribution to mental alertness and focus is often overlooked. Nothing like having a rumbling stomach to drive all other thoughts away and empty the mind!

Practise fasting to bring your attention to the HERE and NOW

In this technique, the area of focus is the lower part of the body, and it helps the mind stay in the here and now. In a similar way in the breath-watching technique, fasting shifts the focus to the body's immediate needs, grounding your attention to the here and now.

By focusing on the sensations in your body—the hunger, the emptiness and the natural rhythm of digestion—you cultivate a sharper sense of awareness. This grounding effect helps quieten the noise in your mind, improves your ability to concentrate and remain focused on tasks at hand. Beyond the physical benefits of improved digestion and a leaner body, fasting provides mental clarity, making it easier to set intentions and stay on track with your goals. Yes, it is a slow process. But quitting will not speed it up. Eat to fill your stomach, not your heart.

Vipassana meditation and exercise are my ways of anchoring to the present. I never miss my 15-minute Vipassana practice each day, nor do I skip my 45-minute exercise session—rain or sunshine. This commitment has helped my mind to quickly return to the present, become less reactive and cultivate a deeper sense of compassion over time. Just like a well-stocked store has all the essentials to keep life running smoothly, these habits ensure that my mental and physical jars are always replenished.

Think of your attention like a shopping cart—what are you filling it with? Are you mindlessly picking up distractions, unnecessary worries and regrets from the past? Or are you choosing the things that truly nourish you—presence, peace and clarity? The checkout counter of life awaits, and only you can decide what is worth keeping in your cart. Choose wisely.

🛒 Checkout Counter

1. Make a commitment to yourself to try one of the techniques mentioned in the chapter or something else entirely. Note what you will do here:

   a.

   b.

   c.

2. How many times in a week will you try the technique and for how long each time?

3. Describe what you went through the first time you tried the technique.

17

Find Joy in Everyday Happiness

Almost every situation in life has parts of it that are good, and parts that are not so good. How you perceive any given situation is largely determined by your outlook towards life and the training you have given your mind. If you choose to see the good, to find the positives, you turn a situation that is seemingly sad and unhappy into one that you derive strength from.

LIFE: A little sunshine, some clouds

and a few rainbows

The Store of Life

Train the mind to find the silver lining

I know! I know!

It is easier said than done. Want to learn some techniques that could help you to train your mind to see the good until it becomes second nature to you?

Maintain a gratitude journal

"Gratitude is the wine for the soul. Go on. Get drunk."
—Rumi

This is a technique often suggested to help you become aware of the things that are good in your life and to be grateful for them. Choose a time during the day when you can dedicate five minutes to list out maximum five things (you can repeat them) you are grateful for. Write them down in a journal. The act of thinking about your life holistically and acknowledging what is good changes your perspective. The act of writing it down cements it and brings these thoughts to the top of your mind. The consistency of doing this every day builds a habit, and as we have seen in the chapter on habits, the outcome is exponential.

List five things you are grateful for in a journal every day

CHALLENGE: See if you can maintain a journal for 66 days at a stretch (to make it a habit)

After a few days (research has shown it takes about 66 days to build a habit though one popular idea suggests that it takes 21 days to solidify a habit), you will notice your outlook has changed; that you are able to find things to be grateful for easily and can stay positive and content for longer periods of time.

The Store of Life 175

As an extension of the gratitude journal, you could even play a game "pass the parcel of gratitude" with your family members or colleagues or friends. Each person is given 30 seconds to mention things they are grateful for and the parcel gets passed on to the next person.

Challenge: See if you can maintain a journal for 66 days at a stretch to build a habit.

Acknowledge everyday joys

"A cheerful heart is good medicine but a crushed spirit dries up the bones."— The Bible

At this moment jot down that one thing that is making you happy.

Notice Everyday joys

CHALLENGE: See if you can put something new in each day

The book that is waiting to be read at home? A new flower from your plant? The baby who smiled at you on the road? The dough that is resting, waiting to be baked into a fresh loaf of bread?

Cultivate the habit of observing and nurturing everyday joy. After all, it is a tough life, and it is the little things that get us through the day.

You can make note of one on a small piece of paper and put it in a jar. Keep filling the jar every time you think of something. After some time, you will notice your jar being full. Open the jar and read through your list to fill your heart with happiness. Remember, when things change inside you, things change around you.

Challenge: See if you can put something new each day.

Wish well for your near and dear ones

What is that one thing in the world that is free to give but priceless to receive?

Kindness.

In a lot of Buddhist meditation techniques, the last activity a meditator performs is to wish well for the world. Some think of the phrase "May all beings be happy" when they are in a calm, positive, meditative state, believing that the peace and contentment they feel at that moment are passed on to the world at large.

One small activity you can do is to sit with your eyes closed every morning and think of your near and dear ones and wish them well. You could either picture their face or take their name in your mind. As you think of them, wish that they be happy and peaceful. Think of them for a few seconds and move on to the next person.

Challenge: Daily, add someone you haven't thought of in the last six days.

It takes a lot of courage to be kind. And you will never regret being kind because kindness is the mark we leave on the world.

Wish well for a stranger

Most people think of their close ones when performing the previous exercise. How about wishing well for perfect strangers too?

When you run into someone—say a cab driver, or the attendant at the cafeteria or a vendor at the market—wish them well. I am sure you can afford kindness even if you are averse to tipping. What can you wish for a perfect stranger?

Certain needs and wants are universal. Wish them lots of money, love and contentment in their lives.

Challenge: Wish happiness for someone who has been rude or unkind to you.

Be kind to the unkind people because they need it most. Yes, in a gentle way you can shake the world.

Thinking about where to start?

A warm smile is a universal language of kindness.

Voice your appreciation

How often have you read epitaphs that sing praises of the departed person?

How many times have you heard someone say something nice about a person when they are not in the same room?

EVERYDAY HAPPINESS

When you admire something about someone, let them know.

CHALLENGE: Admire someone from your own field even when you've a bit envious, and watch the envy melt away!

GREAT PRESENTATION TODAY

YOU'RE SO KIND

THAT WAS A FANTASTIC SHOT!

YOU'VE GOT A GREAT EYE FOR DETAIL

WOW!

YOU'RE AMAZING WITH KIDS

How often do you appreciate someone in your head and never tell them about it? Have you ever stopped and wondered why you do that?

The next time you find yourself admiring something about someone inside your head, voice it out and see what happens.

Challenge: Appreciate someone even when you are a bit envious of them and watch the envy melt away.

Naval Ravikant is a name synonymous with innovation, entrepreneurship and investment success in the Silicon Valley. As one of the most influential angel investors of his generation, he has been involved in some of the biggest tech companies in the world, including Twitter, Uber and Ethereum. He is also known for his profound philosophical insights on wealth, happiness and living a meaningful life, making him a unique figure who bridges the worlds of finance, technology and personal growth.

When you're envious of someone else & feel envy gnawing at your heart..

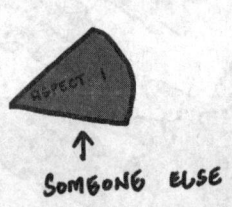

... Imagine them in their entirety and watch the envy melt away

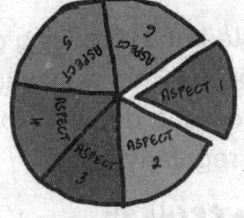

IDEA CREDIT: NAVAL RAVIKANT

He once made a wonderful observation about dealing with envy. He said, "One day, I realized with all these people I was jealous of, I couldn't just choose little aspects of their life. I couldn't say 'I want his body', 'I want her money', 'I want his personality'. You have to be that person. Do you actually want to be that person, with all of their reactions, desires, their family, their happiness level, their outlook on life, their self-image? If you're not willing to do a wholesale, 24/7, 100 per cent swap with who that person is, there is no point in being jealous."

Practise everyday gratitude

Ever wondered why we are often kind and polite to those we hardly know but are most impatient with the ones closest to us? Is it because we take them for granted? Or is it because we have no facade to live up to?

Are you impatient and impolite at your core? Is that your true self?

If you believe you are not that, how do you change the way you interact with people you see daily, be it your immediate family and friends or close acquaintances?

Based on the same principles of expressing gratitude and appreciating someone vocally, this technique deals with planting a seed of gratitude and positivity on a daily basis, with the people we see regularly.

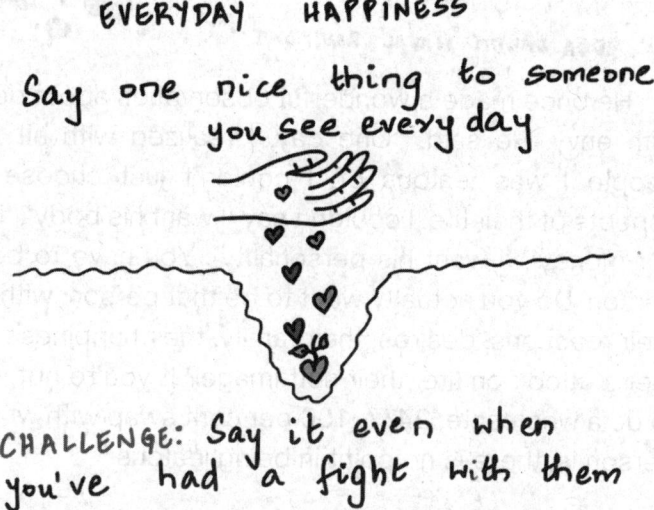

You could set a target of saying one nice thing to them every day and making a mental (or physical) note of it when you do. As with all other habits, once you have done it for a few days in a row, you will see the seed sprouting a few beautiful leaves of positivity, kindness and harmony.

Challenge: Find it within you to appreciate someone even when you have had a fight with them.

🛒 Checkout Counter

1. Close your eyes and think about five people. Visualise each one of them and wish them well. Go ahead, close your eyes. How do you feel? Do you want to pick a time to do this every day?

   a. At what time will you do this exercise each day?

2. List down five things you are grateful for:

   a.

   b.

   c.

   d.

   e.

18

Realise Life is Not a (ZER)(SUM) Game

Theodore Roosevelt once said, "Comparison is the thief of joy."

No wiser words have ever been spoken.

You carefully choose the things that are important to you and invest your time and energy in them. You feel happy with your life basket, until ...

The same person who was content with her life basket...

you run into someone else and start looking at their basket and comparing it to yours. It is almost as if someone else's joy takes away from your own, even though nothing has fundamentally changed in your life basket.

... *feels miserable when she compares her basket with another's*

Has that happened with you?

Zero-sum refers to the situation in game theory in which one person's gain is another person's loss. So, the net change in benefit is zero.

Life, however, is not a zero-sum game; it is abundant and there is enough to keep everyone happy. Someone else's happiness does not take away from your own.

When you do come across a situation which leaves you feeling despondent about the items in your basket of life, it may be useful to take some time out and inspect your own basket of life:

- What are your priorities?
- Are you spending time and energy on the things that are truly important to you?
- Does something need to be taken out or added in your basket of life?

Still can't help comparing your basket with another's?

Do so in a manner that is constructive.

Reflect on what you want from their basket.

Does their successful career bother you?

Don't just sit there and let it continue to bother you.

Focus more on your career and see if you need to change job or need to start adding skills to enhance your career.

- Is your friend's basket full of blissful family life?
- Does that bring you desolation?

See if you have put enough effort into nourishing your relationships and have given it sufficient time.

With this kind of a comparison, the objective is inward-looking—a means to enhance your own basket of life; to constructively investigate another's to see what best practices you can imbibe.

If you are unable to achieve this level of introspection and positivity at a given point in time, it sometimes helps to

Sometimes, examining each item shows you what needs to be added to yours to enrich it

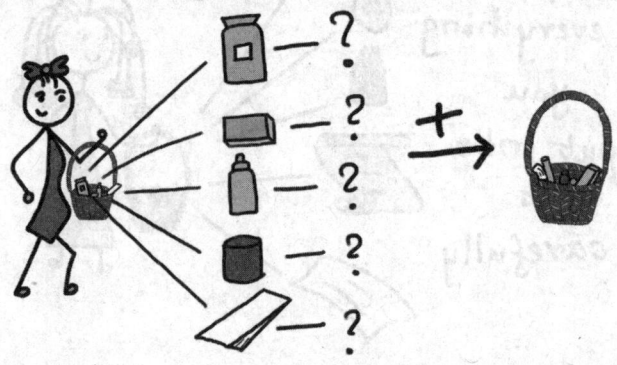

Sometimes, viewing their basket in its entirety changes your view

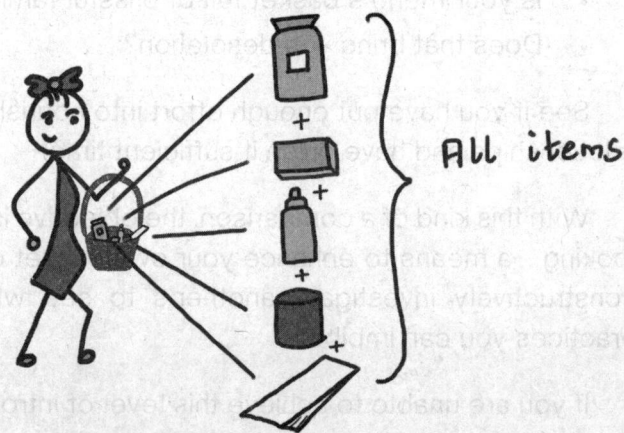

view the other person's basket in its entirety. Most often, it is only one or two elements from their life basket that induces envy or unhappiness in you. Viewing their entire basket with all aspects of their life may help in changing your perspective.

Still not working?

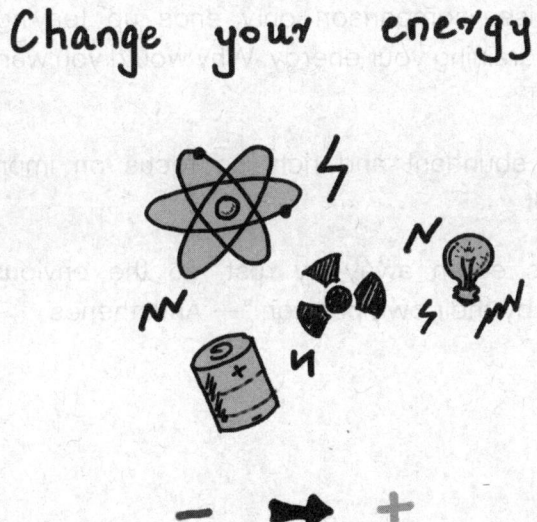

How about shifting your energy from a negative state to a more positive one? Play a game to redirect your focus, immerse yourself in a hobby you are passionate about or tackle a puzzle—anything to engage your mind. These activities not only help to change your perspective but also revitalise your energy.

Your contentment is solely dependent on the "items" you focus on and give your energy to in your basket of life. Comparing someone else's basket of life is good only insofar as to improve yours and enrich it with items you may not have realised were important to you.

Or to realise how much you have to be grateful for.

Otherwise, comparison only ends up leaving you unhappier, draining your energy. Why would you want that for yourself?

Life is abundant and rich, so focus on improving your basket.

"As iron is eaten away by rust, so the envious are consumed by their own passion."— Antisthenes

🛒 Checkout Counter

1. Have you ever felt unhappy when comparing your basket of life with another's?

2. Are there elements in your basket you would like to take away to make you more content?

   a.

   b.

   c.

19

Stay Contented

"Contentment is the only real wealth."— Alfred Nobel

Contentment is an internal compass and measures how happy you truly are on the inside. Happiness is an emotion that is usually characterised by joy, excitement, pride and laughter. It is often a reaction to something, like winning a competition or receiving a gift. Contentment, on the

other hand, is a state of mind that is characterised by peacefulness, gratitude and satisfaction. It is more of an attitude than an emotion, and it can be experienced even in difficult situations.

The premise of this book revolves around living your life fully, intentionally and authentically so that you can cultivate this profound sense of contentment. By nurturing your life basket, filled with experiences, relationships and habits that align with your core values, you create a foundation for enduring happiness. Contentment, then, becomes not just a fleeting feeling but a way of being—a steady companion as you navigate the ebbs and flows of life.

There are three key elements that have been represented in the book in various ways:

Focus on enriching your own basket

The first is to focus on your basket, and your basket alone.

Look at ways and means to enrich your life basket so that you can live a more wholesome life. While you may want to look at someone else's basket to see what can be added to yours, constantly comparing your basket to someone else's is the surest way to ensure you remove all elements of happiness from yours.

The second is to fill your basket of life with items that are relevant to you, depending on the stage of your journey, and giving each item the energy and attention it deserves.

Does your basket look different from how it did five years ago? It is expected to; after all, life evolves. What matters is that it makes sense for where you are in this stage of life.

Does your basket look nothing like anyone else's around, even if they are of a similar age and social standing? That is okay too—only your basket matters, as long as it is authentic to you.

Inspect your basket, deduct items that no longer bring you peace and contentment, and add items that multiply your joy.

Wait!

Don't forget that essential ingredient!

No matter what item you may or may not have, please ensure you have a generous packet of gratitude.

To quote Rabbi Hyman Schachtel, "Happiness is not having what you want. It is wanting what you have."

This does not mean you limit your ambitions or discard your hopes for a better future, it only means being grateful for the things that you do have and knowing that life is transient.

A person who cannot enjoy a sunset is unlikely to enjoy a yacht.

In the end, it is not just about the items in your basket but the spirit in which you carry it. I wish your basket fills you with gratitude, joy and contentment—today, tomorrow and every day.

🛒 Checkout Counter

1. List three things you surely want in your basket of life and think if you give each of those the attention it deserves.

    a.

    b.

    c.

2. List five things you are grateful for:

    a.

    b.

    c.

    d.

    e.

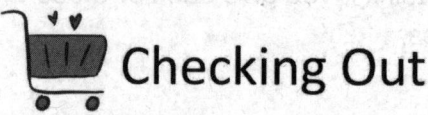 Checking Out

So, here we are at the final checkout point.

How does your basket of life look like?

Ready to plan your ideal basket?

With a set of carefully selected questions, this chapter will help you uncover patterns and design a future of contentment.

One part helps you review, learn from and celebrate the basket you currently have.

The other part is all about the future. You must stop cheating on your future with your past.

You will dream, plan and prepare to get the most out of the coming year and beyond.

Here we go!

The Store of Life

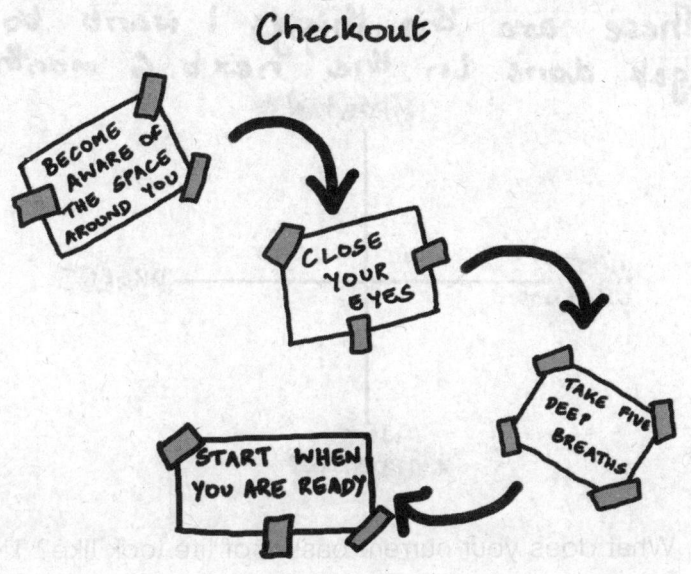

Grab a pen or a pencil, set aside about 20 minutes of uninterrupted focus, and try and have an open and honest mind.

Here are the easy steps:

- Think about the big items that occupy your mind.
- List them in one of these quadrants. This will help you put those thoughts away for a while and focus on your basket.

Now that you have emptied your mind of the big items, please proceed to the next section.

These are the things I want to get done in the next 6 months

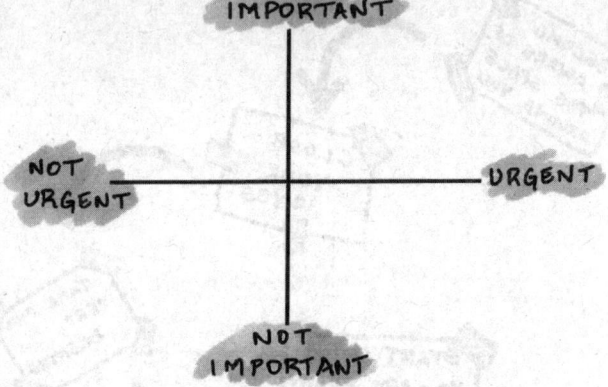

What does your current basket of life look like? Tick all the items that you invest time and energy on:

This is how my Life Basket looks like now

- 🛍️ Personal Life ; Family
- 🛍️ Career ; Studies
- 🛍️ Friends ; Community
- 🛍️ Relaxation
- 🛍️ Hobbies ; Creativity
- 🛍️ Physical Health ; Fitness
- 🛍️ Mental Health ; Self-awareness
- 🛍️ Spirituality
- 🛍️ Others

Tick those that apply

The Store of Life

What does your ideal basket of life look like? What items will bring you the most contentment?

This is how I want my Life Basket to look like

- 🛍 Personal Life; Family
- 🛍 Career; Studies
- 🛍 Friends; Community
- 🛍 Relaxation
- 🛍 Hobbies; Creativity
- 🛍 Physical Health; Fitness
- 🛍 Mental Health; Self-awareness
- 🛍 Spirituality
- 🛍 Others

Tick those that apply

What are the things you will say no to, so that you can say yes to things that truly matter?

I will have the power to say NO to...

...so I can say YES to

Will you make a commitment to learning this year?

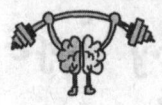 I commit to making a habit of learning

I will make time for learning on:

What are the habits you will inculcate?

I will invest in these 3 habits, knowing it will reap compounding benefits in the future

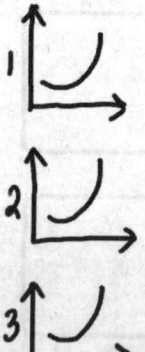

What will you let go?

I will let go of these and ask for help around...

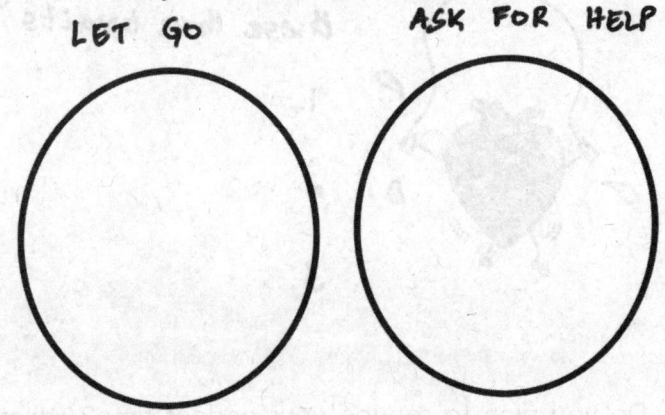

With what will you fill your body, mind and soul jars?

I will add these to each of my jars regularly

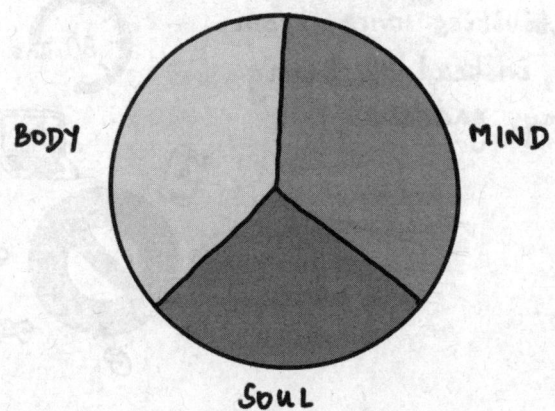

What traits do you wish to develop?

I will consciously practise developing these three traits

1.

2.

3.

Do you plan to reduce your gadget time? What will you do instead?

I will carry out these three activities once I am home, instead of being on my gadgets:

1.

2.

3.

And lastly, will you make a commitment to actively wish well for others and pay it forward?

I promise to wish at least three people well every day.

I will sit in silence for five minutes everyday at ____ time in the morning.

In the end, carry a big basket: one that is open, expansive and ever-evolving. Be willing to embrace new ideas, fresh perspectives and practices that nourish your growth. At the same time, have the courage to let go of what no longer serves you, making space for transformation.

Your basket begins empty, but with every choice, every experience and every lesson, you shape it into something meaningful. Let it hold not just what is easy or familiar, but what is true and necessary.

Follow a plan, not your fleeting moods. Growth is not always comfortable, but it is always worth it. Keep moving forward, keep filling your basket with purpose and trust that the journey itself is the reward.

May you be happy.

cknowledgements

To my dearest Amma and Pappa,

I am because you are. You have been my loudest cheerleaders, my first and most patient teachers and are the unwavering roots that have grounded me while giving me wings to soar. Through you, I have come to understand the depth of fierce, unconditional love—a love that has shaped every part of who I am. I never had to look beyond you for role models—you were always enough.

Thank you, from the bottom of my heart, for being my everything.

To my dear husband Rohith,

You are my first and best reader, my most trusted sounding board and my constant source of encouragement. Every time you read something I have written, I find myself watching your face—eager for your reaction, waiting to see if it resonates with you. Nothing feels ready until it has passed the Ro Litmus Test.

In moments of uncertainty or difficult decisions, while others might wonder what their role models would have done, I find myself asking what you would do—because you always choose what is right.

Thank you for being my unwavering partner and my best friend through these incredible 19 years. I am so deeply grateful for you.

To my dear Kiran Anna,

You were the one who taught me how to ride a bike and were there to pick me up after my first fall. You have stood by my side through so many firsts, and here is another one to add to the list!

Thank you for being my protector, my confidante, and for your unwavering love and steadfast support. I am beholden to you.

To dear Appa and Amma,

Thank you for being my second set of parents, for your quiet, unwavering support and for always standing by me with warmth and kindness. Sitting through the early hours of the morning to read the very first draft of this book from start to finish in one go meant the world to me.

    I am doubly blessed to have you both in my life.

To my dear, ever-dancing Tai Chi master, Sandeep Dhar

Thank you for seeing my potential and setting me up for success in my professional world. You not only guided my career but also planted the seed of this doodle-book, encouraging me to be brave and to write. Your thirst for trying out new things, your ability to dive deep into any topic, always knowing one level more than anyone else, and your endlessly vibrant, ever-expanding life basket have been a constant source of inspiration. Thank you for championing my journey and for being the best boss I could have ever asked for!

My tribe is my fuel,

To dear Baby Aunty, my most loving PR agent, thank you for tirelessly sharing my work on WhatsApp, consolidating feedback and sending it back to me with care. Your support has meant the world to me, my soul friend.

To Priya Sayooj, I am so lucky to have a friend who has known me since I was four! You have always had a kind word for me—whether it is about my writing or my art—and I marvel at the amazing memories you hold in that remarkable mind of yours.

To Jayanth Anna, I am deeply grateful for the connections you helped me make to bring this book to life and for your unwavering encouragement throughout its journey.

To Jennifer Lynch, my leadership coach, and to Lisa Harris, my ex-boss, thank you for being my North Star and for not just holding up a mirror to me, but also polishing it so that my reflection could shine!

Thank you all for being my rock and my inspiration.

To my dear editor Jyotsna Mehta and the team at Om Books International,

They say, when the student is ready, the teacher appears. Similarly, when the writer is ready, the right editor steps in. Finding an editor who not only understands the essence of your writing, but also shares your vision is a rare and beautiful gift from the universe. You made my soul soar after that first phone call when you had received my manuscript.
Thank you for believing in my words, for trusting me with my first book and for being a tough yet fair negotiator. Your thoughtful feedback, impeccably high standards and keen attention to detail have made this book so much better than what it was.

To Shantanu Ray Chaudhuri and everyone else at Om Books International, your faith, encouragement and support have helped birth my dream! Thank you!

To my dear reader,

Something led you to pick up this book, and for that, I am deeply indebted. If even one thought struck a chord or made your life a little better, or if just one doodle brought a smile to your face, it would make it all worthwhile. Thank you!

And last, but most of all, thank you to my *puttani battani* bookworm Advika

I first saw you as a tiny beating semicolon in my first sonogram, and you have now blossomed into an entire, beautiful paragraph. You live and breathe every idea I have shared in these pages. We have been so blessed with a zen-child—calm, gentle, kind, clever, funny and so wonderfully balanced.

You are my semicolon in everyday life, making me pause to reflect, to ensure I am doing what is right and to connect my head, heart and soul every single time.

Thank you for being unapologetically, perfectly you.